DK EYEWITNESS TRAVEL

DUBAI
& ABU DHABI

LARA DUNSTON &
SARAH MONAGHAN

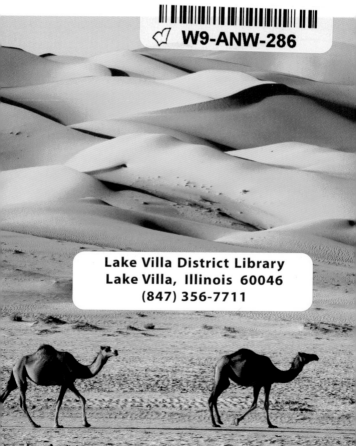

DK | Penguin Random House

Top 10 Dubai and Abu Dhabi Highlights

The Top 10 of Everything

CONTENTS

Dubai and Abu Dhabi Area by Area

Streetsmart

The information in this DK Eyewitness Top 10 Travel Guide is checked regularly. Every effort has been made to ensure that this book is as up-to-date as possible at the time of going to press. Some details, however, such as telephone numbers, opening hours, prices, gallery hanging arrangements and travel information, are liable to change. The publishers cannot accept responsibility for any consequences arising from the use of this book, nor for any material on third party websites, and cannot guarantee that any website address in this book will be a suitable source of travel information. We value the views and suggestions of our readers very highly. Please write to: Publisher, DK Eyewitness Travel Guides, Dorling Kindersley, 80 Strand, London WC2R 0RL, Great Britain, or email travelguides@dk.com

Within each Top 10 list in this book, no hierarchy of quality or popularity is implied. All 10 are, in the editor's opinion, of roughly equal merit.

Front cover and spine *Madinat Jumeirah and the Burj Al Arab hotel in Dubai*
Back cover *Dubai Marina at dusk*
Title page *Riding camels through the desert near Dubai*

Welcome to
Dubai and Abu Dhabi

Dubai and Abu Dhabi are two of the world's most exciting, rapidly changing cities. Packed with soaring skyscrapers, chic shopping malls and luxury resorts, both offer a surfeit of hedonistic pleasures and futuristic style. With Eyewitness Top 10 Dubai and Abu Dhabi, they are yours to explore.

Both these cities have rewritten the record books and established themselves as global icons with recent mega-developments. Dubai's sail-shaped **Burj Al Arab Jumeirah** is one of the Middle East's most instantly recognizable landmarks, now rivalled by the cloud-capped **Burj Khalifa**, the world's tallest building. In Abu Dhabi, the extravagant **Emirates Palace** hotel and monumental **Sheikh Zayed Mosque** have set their own raft of records, with the **Abu Dhabi Louvre** poised to add further lustre to the city's ever-growing array of attractions.

Although modern developments inevitably hog the headlines, both cities – Dubai especially – have an older and much more traditional side. The labyrinthine **souks** of Deira and the historic windtower houses of **Bur Dubai** are a joy to explore, while a ride on Dubai's breezy **creek** is the highlight of any visit. Outside the two cities the desert landscape is spectacular, and is best appreciated with an exhilarating afternoon drive across the sand dunes.

Whether you're coming for a weekend or a week, our Top 10 guide brings together the best of everything the two cities can offer, whether shopping for spices in the backstreets of **Deira** or exploring the futuristic cityscapes of **Dubai Marina** and **Al Maryah Island**. The guide gives tips throughout, from seeking out what's free to avoiding the crowds, plus nine easy-to-follow itineraries designed to help you visit a clutch of sights in a short space of time. Add inspiring photography and detailed maps, and you've got the essential pocket-sized travel companion. **Enjoy the book, and enjoy Dubai and Abu Dhabi.**

Clockwise from top: skyscrapers line Dubai Marina; Burj Khalifa; traditional wooden *dhow* in front of the Dubai Museum; water pool at Sheikh Zayed Mosque; Aladdin shoes in a Bur Dubai souk; desert hotel Anantara Qasr Al Sarab, near the Liwa Oasis; aerial view of the Palm Jumeirah

Exploring Dubai and Abu Dhabi

Both Dubai and Abu Dhabi are very spread out, and away from the old centre of Dubai you won't see much by walking. Fortunately, Dubai's superb modern metro system makes getting around easy, while in Abu Dhabi there are plenty of inexpensive taxis. Whether you have just a couple of days or more time to explore, here are some time-efficient ideas to help you make the most of your visit.

Two Days in Dubai

Day ❶
MORNING
Visit the **Dubai Museum** (see pp14–15; closed Fri mornings) and take in the historic **Al Fahidi** district (see pp18–19). Catch an **abra** across **Dubai Creek** (see pp16–17) and explore the souks in Deira (see pp26–7).
AFTERNOON
Head down to the **Burj Al Arab Jumeirah** (see pp24–5) for afternoon tea (advance booking required), then stroll over to the **Madinat Jumeirah** (see p79) at sunset.

Day ❷
MORNING
Begin with a visit to the soaring **Burj Khalifa** (see pp12–13) for panoramic

views over the city (book your ticket in advance to save money), and then browse the chic shops of the adjacent **Dubai Mall** (see p73).
AFTERNOON
Head out into the sands for a **desert safari** (see p32), starting with a spot of dune bashing. Round off the day with an evening of henna painting, belly dancing and other traditional activities.

Seven Days in Dubai and Abu Dhabi

Day ❶
Start by visiting the **Dubai Museum** (see pp14–15) and then explore the historic **Al Fahidi** (see pp18–19) and **Shindagha** districts (see p16). Towards mid-afternoon head out of the city on a **desert safari** (see p32).

Dubai Mall, the world's largest shopping mall, is packed with stores, food outlets and attractions.

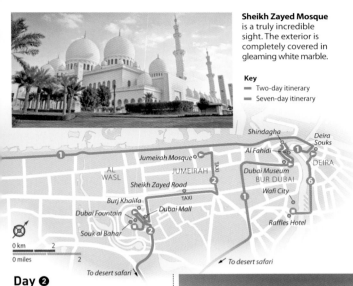

Sheikh Zayed Mosque is a truly incredible sight. The exterior is completely covered in gleaming white marble.

Key
— Two-day itinerary
— Seven-day itinerary

Shindagha
Deira Souks
Al Fahidi
Jumeirah Mosque
DEIRA
JUMEIRAH
TAXI
Dubai Museum
BUR DUBAI
AL WASL
Sheikh Zayed Road
Wafi City
TAXI
Burj Khalifa
Dubai Mall
Dubai Fountain
Raffles Hotel
Souk al Bahar

0 km   2
0 miles   2

↘ *To desert safari*
↙ *To desert safari*

Day ❷
Visit the beautiful **Jumeirah Mosque** *(see pp20–21; closed Fri)*, then take a taxi or metro via **Sheikh Zayed Road** *(see pp70–73)* so that you can admire the skyscrapers en route to the **Dubai Mall** *(see p73)* and **Souk al Bahar** *(see p72)*. Towards sunset, head up the **Burj Khalifa** *(see pp12–13)* for stunning views. End the day watching the spectacular **Dubai Fountain** *(see p71)*.

Day ❸
Take a day trip to explore either the excellent museums and traditional buildings of **Sharjah** *(see p54)* or the marvellous mud-brick forts and oases of idyllic **Al Ain** *(see p54)*.

Day ❹
Head to **Abu Dhabi** *(see pp90–101)* to spend a day exploring the Downtown area and the wonderful **Corniche** *(see pp90–93)*. Book in advance for afternoon tea or dinner at opulent **Emirates Palace** *(see pp30–31)*.

Day ❺
Visit the monumental **Sheikh Zayed Mosque** *(see pp28–9)*, then head down to the **Abu Dhabi Louvre** *(see p97)* before returning to Dubai.

A desert safari is a popular and thrilling way of seeing the desert.

Day ❻
Explore the labyrinthine souks in Deira *(see pp26–7)*. Then head down to the quirky Egyptian-themed **Wafi City** *(see p68)* before ending the day with drinks or a meal in the landmark **Raffles Dubai** *(see p112)*.

Day ❼
Admire the quirky **Ibn Battuta Mall** *(see p83)*, then explore **Dubai Marina** *(see pp82–5)*. Next, head up to the **Burj Al Arab Jumeirah** *(see pp24–5)* for afternoon tea (advance booking required) and explore the stunning **Madinat Jumeirah** *(see p79)*.

Top 10 Dubai and Abu Dhabi Highlights

The entrance to Sheikh Zayed Mosque at dusk, Abu Dhabi

TOP10 Dubai and Abu Dhabi Highlights

The cities of Dubai and Abu Dhabi offer the best of East and West – Arab culture, Bedouin heritage and Islamic architecture, plus sophisticated shopping, dining and hotels. Dubai is set around its creek and skirted with white-sand beaches, while Abu Dhabi is located on a fine corniche.

2 Dubai Museum

Housed in an 18th-century fort, the Dubai Museum, with its fascinating displays, provides a comprehensive introduction to the city (see pp14–15).

1 Burj Khalifa
The world's tallest building and the jewel in the crown of modern Dubai (see pp12–13).

3 Dubai Creek

Crisscrossed by *abras* (water taxis) and *dhows* (old wooden boats) each day, this waterway is Dubai's lifeblood (see pp16–17).

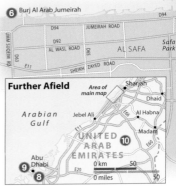

Further Afield

Area of main map

Arabian Gulf

Jebel Ali

Abu Dhabi

Sharjah

Dhaid

Al Habna

Madam

UNITED ARAB EMIRATES

0 km   50
0 miles 50

4 Al Fahidi
The gypsum and coral courtyard houses in this quarter (also known as Bastakiya) were built by Persian merchants who settled here in the 20th century (see pp18–19).

Jumeirah Mosque 5
Not only is this Dubai's most beautiful mosque, it is the only mosque open to non-Muslims. A guided visit to learn about Islamic culture is a must (see pp20–21).

Burj Al Arab Jumeirah 6

This iconic seven-star hotel has long been the defining symbol of Dubai and is still a recognizable landmark, rising high above the coast (see pp24–5).

7 Dubai Souks

Bargain for gold, perfume, spices and textiles, or simply take in the heady atmosphere of Dubai's souks (see pp26–7).

8 Sheikh Zayed Mosque

This vast, snowy-white mosque is topped with myriad domes and minarets. The immense prayer hall is a real highlight (see pp28–9).

9 Emirates Palace

The jaw-dropping display of gold lining the walls and Swarovski crystals dripping from the chandeliers at Abu Dhabi's Emirates Palace hotel make for an impressive sight (see pp30–31).

Desert Escapes 10

A visit to the United Arab Emirates (UAE) is incomplete without a desert experience. Stay at an enchanting resort or take a fun desert safari (see pp32–3).

TOP 10 ⭐ Burj Khalifa and Around

Opened in 2010, the Burj Khalifa is by far the tallest building on the planet (828 m/2,716 ft). Its needle-thin outline soars high above Dubai and is visible from almost 100 km (62 miles) away. The Burj was planned as the centrepiece of the multi-billion-dollar Downtown Dubai development, but only when prompted by Dubai ruler Sheikh Mohammed did architects consider making it the tallest building in the world and a true symbol of Dubai's towering ambitions.

1 Armani Hotel

Occupying several of the Burj's lower floors is the world's first Armani Hotel, showcasing the famous Italian designer's chic minimalist style **(below)**. The hotel boasts some very trendy bars and restaurants, which are open to non-guests for meals and drinks.

2 The Exhibition

Interesting displays scattered around the entrance foyer and en route to the observation decks chart the history of the construction of the Burj, commemorating some of the leading figures involved. A display of fascinating photos also show the tower when it was under construction.

3 Burj Khalifa Lake

The two observation decks offer incredible views for miles around. The views straight down over Downtown Dubai are particularly stunning, with buildings reduced to the size of neat models, clustered around the intense-blue outline of the Burj Khalifa Lake.

NEED TO KNOW
MAP C6

Burj Khalifa: Sheikh Mohammed bin Rashid Boulevard, Dubai; 04 888 8888; open 8:30am–6pm Sat–Thu, 2:30–8:30pm Fri; adm: adults AED 125–500; children AED 95–500; www.burjkhalifa.ae

Armani Hotel: 04 888 3888; www.armanihotels.com

The Address Downtown: 04 436 8888; www.theaddress.com

■ The two observation decks are on floors 124 and 148. Entrance is via the Dubai Mall *(see p73)*. Tickets are cheaper for floor 124 if pre-booked online, but prices rise for sunset. Combination tickets for floors 124 and 148 must be pre-booked and also cost more at sunset.

■ Visit in the evening to watch the Dubai Fountain *(see p71)* perform to music.

4 Souk Al Bahar and Old Town

On the southern side of Burj Khalifa Lake are Souk al Bahar (see p72) and the so-called "Old Town". These mark a change in architectural tone from other nearby buildings with low-rise, sand-coloured Arabian-style design **(right)**.

6 The Exterior

The vast exterior **(left)** is clad in 26,000 individually hand-cut glass panels set into the aluminium and steel curtain wall. Materials were designed to resist scorching summer temperatures.

7 Sheikh Zayed Road

Looking north from the observation deck, the view is dominated by Sheikh Zayed Road's long line of spiky sky-scrapers, although the height of the Burj means that even the tallest is reduced to relative insignificance.

10 At.mosphere

The world's highest bar and restaurant are on Burj Khalifa's 122nd floor. Fine dining and cocktails in the clouds are the theme here (see p75).

5 The Address Downtown

Dominating the view to the southeast of the Burj Khalifa is the huge Address Downtown hotel **(below)**, with its unusual semicircular summit. The hotel made world headlines on New Year's Eve in 2015, when a huge fire engulfed part of the building. Fortunately no one was badly hurt.

8 Jumeirah

Looking west from the Burj, the sea is relatively close at hand, with glimpses of the beach and views over the suburb of Jumeirah (see pp76–81), with its endless sprawl of low, milky-white villas.

9 Burj Al Arab Jumeirah and Beyond

At the far southern end of Jumeirah rises the outline of the Burj Al Arab hotel (see pp24–5). Although it's over 10 km (6 miles) away, the hotel's size means that it's clearly visible. Beyond you can make out the outline of the Palm Jumeirah and the sky-scrapers of the marina.

TOP TEN TOWER FACTS

1 It has more floors (163) than any other building.

2 The world's highest mosque (158th floor) can be found here.

3 Lifts reach speeds of 10 meters per second.

4 Over 12,000 people worked on its construction.

5 A World War II airplane engine was used to test the wind resistance.

6 It takes three months to clean the windows.

7 The total aluminum used is equal to five Airbus 380s.

8 The spire contains over 4,000 tons of steel.

9 Pressurized refuges on every 25th floor provide safety from fires.

10 It is named after the President of UAE, Sheikh Khalifa bin Zayed Al Nahyan.

TOP10 ⭐ Dubai Museum

This cleverly planned museum makes a great starting point for a tour of Dubai. It gives an insight into traditions past and present, and offers a vivid picture of how Dubai has crammed into five decades what most cities achieve in several centuries. Located in the historic creekside Al Fahidi district *(see pp18–19)*, the museum is set within and beneath one of the city's oldest buildings, Al Fahidi Fort. It traces the city's meteoric development from a small desert settlement to the centre of the Arab world for commerce, finance and tourism.

1 Archaeological Finds

Interesting artifacts from excavations of graves that date back to 3,000 BC are on display, including fine copper and alabaster objects and a selection of pottery **(above)**.

2 Desert at Night Exhibitions

Learn how animals that live in the Arabian desert have adapted to cope with the lack of water, extreme temperatures and shortage of food.

3 Multimedia Presentation

An interesting 10-minute film presentation with archive footage explains the development of modern Dubai from 1960 onward. The film takes you through a decade-by-decade pictorial tour of Dubai's transformation over the past 50 years.

4 Old Dubai Souk Dioramas

Holographic technology combined with waxwork figures **(below)**, smells, sounds and archive footage help transport visitors back in time to the creekside souks of half a century ago.

5 Al Fahidi Fort

Constructed in 1787, this fort, with its magnificent watchtower, was built to defend the Emiratis against invasion. Renovated in 1971, it now serves as a city museum.

BEDOUIN CULTURE

Bedu, the Arabic word from which the name Bedouin is derived, means "inhabitant of the desert". Bedouins would move from oasis to oasis by camel and engage in small-scale agriculture. The hardships of the desert have imbued Bedouin culture with a strong honour code and a famous hospitality.

Courtyard Barasti and Windtower House ⑥

The courtyard in the Al Fahidi Fort *(see p19)* houses a *barasti* (date-palm frond) house **(right)** and windtower cooling system, which were both commonly seen in the region as recently as the 1950s.

Floorplan of Dubai Museum

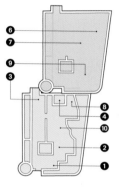

Key to Floorplan

▪ Ground Floor
▪ Basement

⑦ Wooden Dhow

A traditional Arab *dhow* **(above)** is on show at the exit. For celestial navigation, sailors used the *kamal*, a device that determines latitude using the angle of the Pole Star above the horizon.

⑩ Underwater Pearl-Diving Exhibition

This interesting gallery explains the techniques used by pearl divers who wore nose clips so that they could descend to impossible depths.

⑧ Islamic School Dioramas

Young Emiratis recite the lines of the Koran under the watchful eye of their tutor in this reconstruction of a 1950s school.

Bedouin Traditions Display ⑨

A gallery displays the costumes, jewellery, weapons **(right)** and tools of the Bedouin people.

NEED TO KNOW

MAP K2 ▪ Al Fahidi Fort, Al Fahidi St ▪ 04 353 1862 ▪ www.dubai tourism.ae

Open 8:30am–8:30pm Sat–Thu, 2:30–8:30pm Fri

Adm: adults AED 3; children AED 1

▪ A souvenir area at the museum sells traditional Bedouin artifacts.

▪ Retain the flavour of historic Dubai with lunch or a coffee in the shady courtyard of the nearby Arabian Tea House Café *(see p69)*.

TOP 10 ★ Dubai Creek

Dubai Creek, fed by the waters of the Arabian Gulf, is the lifeblood of old and new Dubai. The contrast of traditional wooden *dhows* being unloaded at the wharfage against stunning modern architecture, such as the glass dome-fronted National Bank of Dubai and the giant ball-topped Etisalat building, is fascinating. The two sides of the creek are Deira (north) and Bur Dubai (south) and a walk along either is an ideal way to discover this multi-faceted city. Getting across the creek is easy: the nearest bridge for cars is Maktoum Bridge but the cheapest and most authentic crossing has to be by *abra*.

2 Bur Dubai Waterfront

The Diwan and historic architecture of "Old Dubai" are best enjoyed from the Deira side of the creek: here you can see windtowers, minarets and the domes of the Grand Mosque.

3 Shindagha Heritage

In the Shindagha area near the mouth of the creek you will find the restored house and museum of the late ruler Sheikh Saeed Al Maktoum (see p67) and the Heritage and Diving Village (see p66), which showcases Arabian culture.

1 The Diwan

With its modern white windtowers and imposing wrought-iron gates, the Diwan **(above)**, or Ruler's Office, is an impressive and important building (see p65).

Map of Dubai Creek

4 Creekside Park

A wonderful expanse of parkland, Creekside Park stretches along the water's edge. Walk its length and enjoy the vistas or take a half-hour cable car ride along the length of the entire park.

NEED TO KNOW

MAP K1–K4

Creekside Park: 04 336 7633; open 8am–11pm Sun–Wed, 2–11:30pm Thu–Sat; Adm: AED 5; www.dm.gov.ae

Abra Crossing: Route 1: 5am–midnight, Route 2: 24 hours; AED 1 each way

Al Mansour Dhow: opposite Radisson Blu Hotel, Baniyas Road; 04 222 7171; departs at 8:30pm daily

Bateaux Dubai: 04 399 4994; departs at 7:45pm daily; www.jaresorts hotels.com

Creek Cruises: 04 393 9860; www.creekcruises.com

■ By night, admire the illuminated *dhows* as they glide along the creek.

■ If you need a refreshment in the area, stop for a cooling fresh juice at the stall by the entrance to the Textile Souk (see p27).

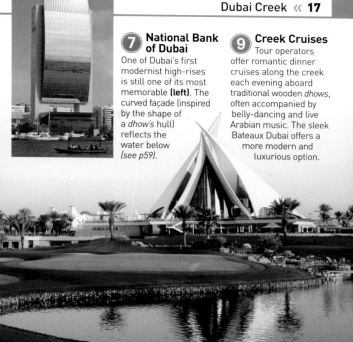

7 National Bank of Dubai

One of Dubai's first modernist high-rises is still one of its most memorable **(left)**. The curved façade (inspired by the shape of a *dhow's* hull) reflects the water below *(see p59)*.

9 Creek Cruises

Tour operators offer romantic dinner cruises along the creek each evening aboard traditional wooden *dhows*, often accompanied by belly-dancing and live Arabian music. The sleek Bateaux Dubai offers a more modern and luxurious option.

5 Dubai Creek Golf Club

The Dubai Creek Golf Club building **(above)** is one of the city's most unusual modernist landmarks, with glass-fronted façades nestled beneath three spiky white "sails" *(see p60)*.

6 Dhow Wharfage

Stroll beside the creek along Baniyas Road, where colourfully painted wooden *dhows* **(below)** are moored and boats arrive from Iran, Oman and the rest of the UAE.

8 Abra Trips

Abras are flat-bottomed, open-sided water taxis and are a breezy way to travel the creek. Cram in with other passengers – the *abras* carry 40,000 people per day – and enjoy the views.

HISTORY OF DUBAI CREEK

Once a tiny fishing settlement sprawled around the mouth of the creek, Dibei, as it was known in the 16th century, owes its existence to the 14-km (9-mile) Dubai Creek, which led into a natural harbour and established itself as a flourishing hub for entrepôt trade.

10 Marsa al Seef

Stretching along the Bur Dubai waterfront, Marsa al Seef is the biggest development in the history of the creek. Due to open in 2017, it will have a traditional souk, *abra* station, shops, cafés and a museum.

TOP 10 ⭐ Al Fahidi

The beautifully restored old Al Fahidi quarter (also known by its old name of Bastakiya) gives a picturesque glimpse into the city's past, in sharp contrast to the futuristic architecture found elsewhere. As you wander the maze of shady streets and alleys, traditional windtower houses with elegant courtyards can be seen in sand, stone, coral and gypsum. The buildings have been restored to their original state, with Arabesque windows, decorative gypsum panels and screens. This area is home to art galleries, museums and cafés.

1 Traditional Architecture
The need to remain cool prompted the vernacular style of the windtower courtyard houses. Thick walls and narrow windows with intricate Arabesque designs are featured.

2 Majlis Gallery
Named after the word for a meeting place in Arabic, Majlis is a bijou art gallery built around a beautifully converted whitewashed Arabic house with a central garden. It houses the works of local Emirati and expat artists, and features original pottery, ceramics, crafts and jewellery *(see p38)*.

3 Coins Museum
The Coins Museum showcases Arabian money **(left)** through the ages. Almost 500 coins are on display from Ummayad to Ottoman times, with touchscreens providing fascinating historical information.

4 Sheikh Mohammed Centre for Cultural Understanding
This pioneering centre aims to give visitors and expats a deeper understanding of Emirati culture. A number of activities are available, including walking tours of Al Fahidi *(see p55)* and regular "cultural" breakfasts and lunches.

5 Coffee Museum
This museum reveals the history of the region's favourite drink. Exhibits include old-fashioned grinders, coffee pots and antique tins **(above)**, and you can try a cup of Arabian-style coffee.

6 Old City Wall
Restoration work of the original 200-year-old city wall **(left)** has drawn attention to the history of this section of the city as a crucial defensive zone.

7 Bastakiah Nights Restaurant

With its courtyard setting, this restaurant boasts an Arabian atmosphere best experienced after dusk. The restored building **(left)** has been traditionally furnished, with authentic Arabic and Emirati food served inside or on the rooftop.

NEED TO KNOW

MAP K2

Coins Museum: 04 515 5035; open 8am–1pm & 5–8pm Sun–Wed, 9am–1pm Thu

Sheikh Mohammed Centre for Cultural Understanding: 04 353 6666; open 8am–5pm Sun–Thu, 9am–1pm Sat; www.cultures.ae

Coffee Museum: 04 353 8777; open 9am–5pm Sat–Thu; www.coffee museum.ae

Bastakiah Nights Restaurant: 04 353 7772; open 11am–11pm

■ Visit Al Fahidi late in the day when the golden light and long shadows add to the atmosphere.

■ For lunch, the Arabian Tea House Café offers healthy light meals and snack options – fresh soup and salad (see p69).

10 Arabian Tea House Café

Located in a traditional courtyard of an Al Fahidi house, this café is a great spot to sit amid flowering bougainvillea and enjoy lunch (see p69).

WINDTOWERS

The most distinctive architectural element of Arabian houses in the early 20th century, windtowers (*barjeel*) were designed to create natural ventilation. With four open sides, each of which was hollowed into a concave v-shape, windtowers deflected the air down, cooling the rooms below. Water was thrown on the floor beneath the tower to cool the house further.

8 Al Fahidi Fort

An interesting museum that provides insight into the history, culture and heritage of Dubai. The original walls of the fort were built from coral and shell rubble (see pp14–15).

9 XVA Gallery, Café and Hotel

Contemporary art is on display in galleries off the courtyard of this restored traditional house **(right)**. It is also home to a café and hotel (see p38).

TOP 10 ⭐ Jumeirah Mosque

Dubai's culture is rooted in Islam, a fact that touches all aspects of everyday life. Virtually every neighbourhood has its own mosque, but the jewel in the crown is undoubtedly Jumeirah Mosque. This fine example of modern Islamic architecture was built in 1998. It is a dramatic sight set against blue skies and is especially breathtaking at night, when it is lit up and its artistry is thrown into relief. Built of smooth white stone, the mosque, with its elaborately decorated twin minarets and majestic dome, is a city landmark and an important place of worship.

1 The Hajj
Every able-bodied Muslim is expected to make the annual pilgrimage to Mecca, in Saudi Arabia, once. Each year millions of Muslims from all over the globe do so to be forgiven of sins, to pray and to celebrate the glory of Allah **(below)**.

3 Mosque Architecture
With its vast central dome **(right)**, this mosque is inspired by the Anatolian style. The exterior is decorated in geometric relief over the stonework.

2 Ramadan
During the holy month of Ramadan (the ninth month of the Islamic calendar), Muslims abstain from food, drink and other physical needs from dawn till sunset. This is a time for purification and to focus on Allah.

NEED TO KNOW
MAP E4 ■ Jumeirah Road, Jumeirah ■ 04 353 6666
Mosque Tours: 10am Sat–Thu, meet by the entrance to the mosque 10 minutes in advance (no booking required); adm: AED 20, under 12s free

■ Close to the mosque, the Lime Tree Café *(see p81)* serves sandwiches, cakes and coffee.

■ The mosque tours are intended to help visitors gain a real understanding of the Islamic faith, so make the most of the question time to find out what you would like to know. Photography is permitted inside.

■ Each tour lasts about 75 minutes. Admission includes water, dates, Arabic coffee, tea and traditional pastries.

⑤ Prayers
The *adhan* (call to prayer) rings out from the minarets five times a day – all able Muslims must supplicate themselves **(above)** to Allah by praying on a *musalla* (traditional mat).

⑥ Five Pillars of Islam
The "Five Pillars of Islam" are: *Shahadah*, the belief in the oneness of God; *Salat*, the five daily prayers; *Zakat*, alms-giving; *Siyam*, self-purification and *Hajj*, the pilgrimage to Mecca.

⑨ Mihrab
The *mihrab* **(below)** is the niche in the wall of this and every mosque that indicates the *qibla*, the direction a Muslim should face when praying. This *mihrab* gives the impression of a door or a passage to Mecca.

④ "Open Doors, Open Minds" Guided Tour
Jumeirah Mosque is the only mosque in Dubai open to the public. The "Open Doors, Open Minds" interactive guided mosque tour, run by the Sheikh Mohammed Centre for Cultural Understanding *(see p18)*, offers an opportunity to admire the subtle interior decoration and to gain insight into Islam.

⑦ Minarets
Two minarets **(above)** crown this mosque. The height of the tallest one – the highest point of the "House of Allah" – is determined by how far the call to prayer should be heard.

⑧ Minbar
The *minbar* is the pulpit from which the *Imam* (leader of prayer) stands to deliver the *khutba* (Friday sermon).

⑩ Mosque Etiquette
Dubai may be very cosmopolitan, but in keeping with mosque etiquette, you must dress conservatively to enter. No shorts or sleeveless tops for either gender; women must wear a headscarf. Remove your shoes before entering.

Following pages The beautiful interior of the Sheikh Zayed Mosque

TOP 10 ⭐ Burj Al Arab Jumeirah

So recognizable that it instantly became an international symbol for modern Dubai, the Burj Al Arab Jumeirah (meaning "Arabian tower"), completed in 1999, is an exclusive all-suite hotel. With its helipad on the 28th floor and a restaurant seemingly suspended in mid-air, it is a place of sheer decadence. At a soaring 321 m (1,053 ft), it also takes the trophy for being the world's tallest all-suite hotel. Set on its own artificial island against the backdrop of the turquoise waters of the Gulf, it is dazzling white by day and rainbow-coloured by night, when its façade is used as a canvas for spectacular light displays.

NEED TO KNOW

MAP C1 ■ Jumeirah Rd, Dubai ■ 04 301 7777 ■ www.jumeirah.com

Al Mahara: open 12:30–3pm, 7pm–midnight

Skyview Bar: open noon–2am

■ In order to enter the hotel, you must have a reservation for a meal, cocktails or afternoon tea. To do this, call the hotel at 04 301 7600 or email BAArestaurants@jumeirah.com. The most affordable options are drinks at Gold On 27 and at Scape Restaurant & Bar, or food at Bab Al Yam.

■ The dress code at Gold On 27 and Scape Restaurant & Bar is "stylish chic", and smart casual dress is required at Bab Al Yam.

1 Talise Spa
Perched on the 18th floor, Talise Spa is an idyllic retreat with soothing ocean views. The beautiful decor is reminiscent of baths used by ancient Middle Eastern civilizations. There are panoramic views from the infinity pools.

2 The Exterior
The shore-facing façade of the Burj is covered by what looks like stretched translucent fabric. This is Teflon-coated woven glass fibre. It is the first time such technology has been used in this way in any building worldwide.

3 Skyview Bar
With its sky-high location, this rooftop bar offers the most amazing vistas of the shimmering coastline. The bar – a must for cocktails at sunset – is reached by an express panoramic lift.

4 Lobby
The lobby is an airy space of marbles, mosaics and hand-crafted carpets in swirling patterns. There is an impressive multi-hued dancing fountain.

5 The Atrium
The vast gold-leaf-covered columns and many layers of floors rising up from the lobby **(above)** give a strange dizzying sensation.

10 The Helipad

Jutting out of the building's summit, the Burj's iconic helipad (below) has featured in numerous commercials. It is also a unique wedding venue, and once hosted a game of tennis between Andre Agassi and Roger Federer.

6 Suites

The 202 amazing duplex suites (above) are equipped with the latest remote technology, plus in-suite check-in and personal butler service. The two Royal Suites offer unsurpassed luxury, even including a private cinema.

7 Fish Tanks

The lobby boasts a pair of enormous tropical aquariums. They are so large that members of the hotel staff have to put on diving suits in order to clean them out.

8 Nathan Outlaw at Al Mahara

At the base of the tower, this lavish but intimate restaurant is centred on a circular aquarium. Dine on superb seafood from a menu devised by Michelin-starred chef Nathan Outlaw.

9 Architectural Inspiration

The billowing sail of the Arabian *dhow* was the inspiration for this contemporary creation (below). Access for guests is by helicopter or via Rolls Royces on the causeway.

THE CONSTRUCTION

The Burj Al Arab Jumeirah is said to be one of the most expensive buildings ever constructed – an estimated $2 billion was spent on it, though the full cost has never been revealed. Built on its own artificial island (which took three years to reclaim), the Burj al Arab Jumeirah rises to a height of 321 m (1,053 ft); it was the world's tallest hotel until 2007. Inside, the building's dazzling decor incorporates over 30 types of marble and 8,000 sq m (86,111 sq ft) of shimmering 22-carat gold leaf ornamentation.

Dubai Souks

Shopping in Dubai is a shopaholic's dream, with almost nothing that cannot be bought here, but away from the air-conditioned marble-floored shopping malls is another experience: the souks. Many of these, such as the gold, textile and spice souks clustered beside the creek, date back to Dubai's beginnings as a palm-fringed trading port. Exploring their warren-like alleyways is a delight. Generally, each type of stall, be it spices, crafts, perfumes or clothing, are located close together, making it easy to spot a good deal. Bring cash and keep in mind that bargaining is expected.

1 Naif Rd Souk, Deira

A kitsch faux desert fort houses this traditional-style souk with everything from cheap clothes and fake designer accessories to children's toys.

3 Deira Covered Souk

This souk feels more Indian than Arabic, with a medley of merchandise offered: colourful textiles, spices, kitchenware, clothes and henna.

2 Gold Souk

This souk gleams with gold **(below)**, silver and gems. Prices are competitive; dealers come in from around the globe and strict regulations are followed.

VISIT TO A TAILOR'S

Dubai is a wonderful place for tailoring, with an incredible array of textiles being widely available. Various tailors' shops can be found around the Textile Souk, but also elsewhere in Satwa and Bur Dubai. Most tailors will make an exact replica from the original item or a photograph, or you can select from their range of pattern books.

Map of the Dubai Souks

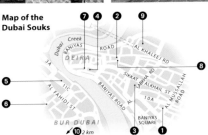

4 Deira Grand Souk

Sprawling behind the Spice Souk, Deira's Al Souk Al Kabeer ("Big Souk") boasts hundreds of shoebox shops clad in coral-stone façades. The cute little Al Arsa Courtyard at the back is especially pretty.

7 Deira Spice Souk

This tiny souk is a real sensory delight. You can purchase aromatic frankincense and myrrh (with charcoal burners for them), plus an array of spices **(left)** such as cloves, cardamom and cinnamon. Iranian saffron is particularly good value, too.

NEED TO KNOW

Open 10am–10pm (some souks shut at 1:30pm to attend the prayers) ■ www.dubai-tourism.ae

■ Bargaining is expected. Start at half of the initial price and haggle until you reach a compromise.

■ Tax-free prices in Dubai make luxury items such as perfume and electronic goods highly affordable.

■ Around the Bur Dubai souks are good-value Indian restaurants.

9 Dubai Food Souk

Great piles of colourful fruit and vegetables (especially dates), huge hunks of meat and heaps of ocean-fresh hammour and shark are just some of the foodstuffs on offer at this bustling souk.

10 Karama Souk

This souk offers "copy" items, especially watches and handbags. The quality of much of the products, although fake, is very good **(below)**.

5 Bur Dubai Textile Souk

Beautifully restored, this creekside souk **(above)** is covered by an arched pergola. It makes for an atmospheric walkway lined with money lenders and little stalls selling reels of cloured cloth.

6 Bur Dubai Meena Bazaar

Be warned, a visit here may necessitate a trip to a tailor. Wonderful fabrics from all over the world, in every colour and texture imaginable (silks, satins, brocades, linens and more), are laid out before you.

8 Deira Perfume Souk

Fascinating shops sell heavy exotic scents like jasmine, oudh, amber and rose, and will also mix individual "signature scents". Traditional Arabian attars are for sale alongside well-known Western brands.

⭐ Sheikh Zayed Mosque

Standing guard over the city, the monumental Sheikh Zayed Mosque is the largest mosque in the UAE. It has room for 40,000 worshippers and attracts vast crowds during festivals such as Eid. Built between 1996 and 2007, the mosque was the brainchild of the late president of the UAE, Sheikh Zayed bin Sultan Al Nahyan. Vast quantities of marble, gold, semiprecious stones and crystals were used in the construction, while the Pan-Islamic design unites styles including Persian, Mughal and Moorish.

1 The Exterior
The outline of the mosque, with its four great minarets, dominates all approaches to the city. Covered in snowy-white Sivec marble from Macedonia, the building is topped with over 100 domes.

4 The Prayer Hall Carpet
The floor of the main prayer hall is covered in a single vast carpet, the largest in the world. Made in Iran, the carpet is well over 5,000 sq m (53,819 sq ft) in size, weighs around 35 tonnes and contains an estimated 2.26 million knots.

5 The Prayer Hall Chandelier
Hanging magnificently above the centre of the prayer hall is the largest of the mosque's seven huge chandeliers. Produced in Germany, this is the third biggest chandelier in the world – measuring some 10 m (33 ft) wide and 15 m (49 ft) high. It was made using over a million Swarovski crystals.

6 The Minarets
Four minarets stand at each corner of the courtyard, rising some 107 m (351 ft) high. The design of the minarets fuses Mamluk, Ottoman and Fatimid styles from Turkey and Egypt, symbolizing the diverse traditions of Islamic architecture around the world.

2 The Prayer Hall
The cavernous main prayer hall **(above)** is an extravagant showpiece of decoration and design, supported by 96 marble-clad columns inlaid with mother of pearl. The hall is capable of holding over 7,000 worshippers.

The Entrance 3
Entrance to the mosque is via a grand white arcade **(right)**, with lines of gold-topped pillars to either side. The entrance is fronted by long pools of water.

(8) The Qibla

The prayer hall's *qibla* wall (indicating the direction of Mecca) has a golden alcove set into the wall surrounded by the 99 names of Allah written in traditional Kufic calligraphy **(left)**.

SHEIKH ZAYED

Former ruler of Abu Dhabi and "Father of the UAE", Sheikh Zayed bin Sultan Al Nahyan (1918–2004) became leader of Abu Dhabi in 1966 following a peaceful coup against his elder brother. He instigated a programme that rapidly launched the city's transformation from Arabian backwater to global city. In 1971, he also became the first president of the newly formed UAE. Famed for his generosity, Zayed remains a revered figure throughout the country.

(10) The Minbar

Sitting alongside the *qibla* alcove is the small *minbar* (pulpit), from which sermons are given during Friday Prayers **(below)**.

(7) The Courtyard

The vast courtyard **(above)** has space for 30,000 worshippers and is dazzlingly bright during the day. The floral mosaic, picked out in marble on the floor, is said to be the largest in the world.

(9) Tomb of Sheikh Zayed

Outside the mosque is the tomb of Abu Dhabi's former ruler, Sheikh Zayed bin Sultan Al Nahyan. The tomb is as understated as the rest of the mosque is ornate.

NEED TO KNOW

MAP V3 ■ Khaleej al Arabi and Sheikh Rashid bin Saeed streets ■ 02 419 1919 ■ www.szgmc.ae/en

Open 9am–10pm Sat–Thu, 4:30–10pm Fri

Free guided tours: 10am, 11am & 5pm Sat–Thu (also 2pm & 7pm Sat), 5pm & 7pm Fri

■ Visitors must remove shoes and cover arms and legs. Women are asked to wear a robe and headscarf (provided free).

■ The 5pm Sunset Tour is a nice time of day to see the mosque, and the building also looks spectacular after dark, with a unique lighting system designed to reflect the phases of the moon.

■ For refreshment head to the nearby Souk Qaryat al Beri (see p97), with its many cafés and restaurants.

TOP 10 ★ Emirates Palace

The stupendous Emirates Palace hotel dominates Downtown Abu Dhabi's southwestern side. Opened in 2005 to rival Dubai's Burj Al Arab Jumeirah, the hotel cost a reputed $3 billion and is built on the grandest of scales, stretching for well over a kilometre along its own exclusive beach. The hotel's majestic red-sandstone exterior, topped with rippling domes and surrounded by gushing fountains, is guaranteed to impress. Even more spectacular, however, is the lavish interior, a dazzling, shimmering vision of marble, gold leaf and opulent decorative features.

NEED TO KNOW

MAP N1 ■ The Corniche, Abu Dhabi ■ 02 690 9000 ■ www.emirates palace.com

■ Officially you need an advance reservation to get into the hotel. However, the lobby is open to the public. For reservations email: guestrelation@ emiratespalace.ae

■ For a soothing evening, Emirates Palace Spa offers an array of excellent spa escapes, such as the signature 24 Carat Gold Radiance Facial.

■ For afternoon tea or a cup of coffee, call into Al Majlis coffee lounge or the Viennese-style café. For lunch or dinner, try Mezzaluna (02 690 7999; 12:30–3pm & 7–11pm) or Sayad (see p95).

① Swarovski Crystal Chandeliers

You'll notice the abundant use of chandeliers throughout the hotel – at Emirates Palace, they're used like light bulbs and appear to be sparkling in every single room.

② Triumphant Arch

Before entering Emirates Palace you'll be dazzled by a majestic pink Triumphant Arch gate with a dome on top and a long and grand driveway **(left)**. The gate is usually closed but opened for royalty and dignitaries on special occasions.

③ Majlis with Arabian Horse Mural

The most impressive of the many plush public spaces here is the *majlis* (meeting area). It has a blue ceiling with frescoes and a magnificent mural of Arab stallions.

④ Emirates Palace Theatre

Emirates Palace has given Abu Dhabi its first theatre, a remarkable venue that is the largest in the UAE. The packed programme includes Russian ballet, Arabic orchestra concerts and musical shows like "The Spirit of the Dance".

Palace Suites 5

Emirates Palace has 302 plush rooms and 92 sumptuously decorated Khaleej and Palace Suites. On the fifth floor is a reception for kings and heads of state and on the eighth are suites designed especially for the Gulf Rulers. The Saudi suite **(right)** even has its own barbershop.

9 Palace Gardens and Fountains

The exterior of the palace **(left)** adopts traditional Arabian architectural elements and is painted to reflect the variations in colour of the Arabian sands. It is beautifully enhanced by its landscaped gardens and stunning fountains.

10 Algerian Sand Beach

The white sand of the 1.3-km- (1-mile-) long beach was imported from Algeria. A popular beach for swimming and cricket before Emirates Palace was built, it was felt the sand wasn't soft enough for royal feet.

6 Domes

There are 114 domes here. The most stunning is the Grand Atrium dome, decorated with silver and gold glass mosaic tiles and a gold finial at its apex.

7 Petrified Palm Trees

There are 8,000 trees within the hotel. The date palm, which is a national icon, can be seen everywhere. Some of the palm trees, petrified to preserve their natural beauty, look real and are very impressive.

8 Gold-Plated Lobby

The opulence of the lobby's gold interior **(left)** is dazzling. Until Emirates Palace was built, Abu Dhabi was a modest city. It was here that the city's wealth was ostentatiously put on display for the first time.

ON A SCALE LIKE NO OTHER

The Emirates Palace is spread over 1 million sq m (10 million sq ft), with over 300 rooms, around 2,000 staff from 50 different countries, 114 domes, 1,002 chandeliers, two helipads and a ballroom capable of accommodating more than 2,500 people. It is claimed even hotel staff sometimes get lost in the endless corridors.

Desert Escapes

The Emirates' desert is sublime in parts and a trip here is incomplete without experiencing its myriad textures and colours. Not far out of the cities, camels graze on desert grass. If you don't have a 4WD and off-road driving skills, the best way to experience the desert is at the magical desert resorts Al Maha or Bab Al Shams. Or take a desert safari, which allows you to tick off a range of experiences you otherwise would not get a chance to do. If you have time, stay overnight, sleep under the stars and enjoy the silence.

LIWA OASIS

The most spectacular desert scenery can be enjoyed at Liwa Oasis, just a few hours drive from Abu Dhabi. The sand dunes here are the largest in the UAE. Beautifully coloured in pretty shades of peach and apricot, the sand dunes look at their best shortly after sunrise or just before sunset.

3 Ballooning
Drifting over the desert in a hot-air balloon **(right)** is an incredible experience. Balloon Adventures Emirates fly over the Dubai Desert Conservation Reserve.

1 Desert Safaris
Tour agencies like Arabian Adventures organize desert safaris. These may include a thrilling desert drive in a 4WD, falconry displays, camel rides, Arabic buffets and belly dancing.

4 Dubai Desert Conservation Reserve
Experience the unspoiled desert at this reserve, with dunes and rare wildlife, including oryx and mountain gazelle. Visit on a day tour or stay at the Al Maha resort.

5 Al Maha Resort
Book a romantic tent-like luxury suite, and get your own plunge pool with the golden desert as your "backyard" (see p117).

2 Bab Al Shams Desert Resort
The palm-shaded gardens and trickling ponds make this resort **(above)** enchanting. A wonderful infinity pool overlooks the desert (see p117).

6 Belly Dancing

Belly dancing is known as Oriental dancing in the Middle East, and it has a long history. Try to pick up some moves from the dancer at the desert safari – she may even pull you up for a dance.

8 Dune Bashing

Experience an exhilarating "dune bashing" session – a white-knuckle 4WD desert drive crashing over huge dunes and wheel-spinning out of dips **(above)**. It is not for the faint-hearted.

NEED TO KNOW

Arabian Adventures: 04 303 4888/343 9966 (Dubai), 02 691 1711 (Abu Dhabi); open 9am–6pm; from AED 250; www.arabian-adventures.com

Balloon Adventures Emirates: 04 388 4044; open Sep–May; www.ballooning.ae

Dubai Desert Conservation Reserve: www.ddcr.og

Abu Dhabi Falcon Hospital: Sweton Rd; tours 10am & 2pm Sun–Thu; www.falcon hospital.com

■ Unless you want to experience the scorching heat, it is best to visit the desert in spring, autumn or winter.

7 Bedouin Feast

Tuck into a delicious Arabic buffet, such as the Bedouin feast at Bab Al Shams' Al Hadheerah Desert Restaurant. You can experience local specialities including roasted baby camel.

9 Falconry

Falconry is one of the UAE's most cherished desert traditions, with magnificent birds of prey – falcons **(left)**, hawks and eagles – swooping across the sands. Displays are offered in various places including the Al Maha and Bab Al Shams resorts.

10 Camel Riding

Become friendly with this local beast of burden. Nothing is quite like a camel ride **(above)** along spectacular dunes at sunset. Ride a camel at the Heritage and Diving Village in Dubai *(see p66)*.

The Top 10
of Everything

The atrium at Burj Al Arab Jumeirah, Dubai

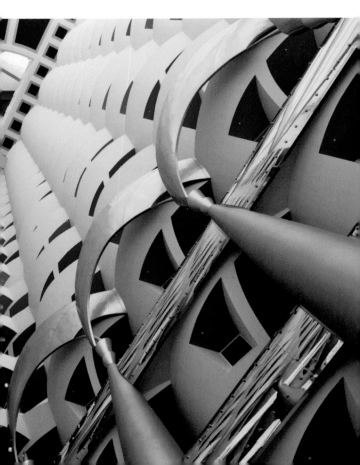

Culture and Tradition

An Emirati man training a falcon

1 Falconry
In the past, falcons were used by Bedu to capture small birds and hares. Today, Emirati men still train their falcons daily. Some desert resorts and safaris have falconry displays *(see p33)*.

2 Traditional Dress
Women wear a black *abaya* (a cloak-like dress) and a black *shayla* (scarf) to cover their hair. Men wear a white *dishdasha* (robe) and a white or checked *gutra* (head scarf) with a black *agal* (cord) to hold it in place.

3 The Camel
A mainstay of the Bedouin's nomadic life, the camel enabled Bedouin tribes to move their possessions from coastal villages to inland oases. Camel's milk quenched their herders' thirst when water wasn't found, while the fur was used to make tents, textiles, rugs, bags and cloaks. Camel's milk is more nutritious than cow's milk, and you can buy it at local supermarkets

in Dubai and Abu Dhabi. You can ride a camel at the Heritage and Diving Village in Dubai *(see p66)*.

4 Fishing and the *Dhow*
Historically, fishing, pearl diving and building *dhow* (boats) were the main occupations along the coastal settlements. Today, Emiratis still use the old wooden *dhow* boats for fishing, trading and tours. Visit *dhow*-building wharfs in Deira *(see p61)*.

5 Bedouin Society
The seminomadic lifestyle of the Bedu tribes – most of whom spent the harsh summers inland at the cool date-palm oases and their winters fishing by the sea – is a source of pride for Emiratis. Visit the Heritage Villages in Dubai *(see p66)* and Abu Dhabi *(see p92)* for a glimpse into the Bedouin culture.

6 Poetry, Dance and Song
Emirati poetry takes many forms, from the romantic *baiti* style to the vernacular *nabati* poetry. Wedding processions are an occasion for song and dance. Songs and group dances such as the *ayyalah* and *liwa* celebrate bravery in war and at sea. Enjoy traditional performances at the Heritage and Diving Village *(see p66)* and in Downtown Dubai during Eid and the Dubai Shopping Festival *(see p39)*.

7 The Arabian Horse
Beloved by the Bedouin for their elegance and valued for their strength and sturdiness, the Arabian horse is one of the world's oldest and purest of breeds due to the Bedouin's careful breeding.

Camel with a bright saddle blanket

Appreciate the beauty of the Arabian horse at the Heritage and Diving Village *(see p66)* during both Eid and the Dubai Shopping Festival.

8 Pearling

Up until the 1920s, pearling was Dubai's major source of income. By the turn of the 20th century the city had well over 1,000 pearling boats employing most of the city's men during pearling season.

9 The Date Palm

Dates were essential for desert survival. They were used to create *tamr*, a preserve,

which helped sustain the Bedu over long journeys. There are over 50 date varieties in the UAE. The Dubai Food Souk *(see p59)* is the best place to shop for dates.

A basket of dates

10 Henna

Intricate henna patterns were painted on pottery across the Middle East in around 9000 BC (the start of the Neolithic period). Today, Emirati women have henna designs painted on their hands and feet for weddings and other events. Get henna designs at "henna tents" in shopping malls.

Henna designs being applied

MOMENTS IN HISTORY

Death of Sheikh Zayed

1 5110 BC: Abu Dhabi settlement
Date stones on Dalma Island and flint tools on Merawah Island attest to human life in Abu Dhabi in 5110 BC.

2 AD 700: Islam arrives
The Umayyads bring Islam to Arabia.

3 1507: European traders reach the Gulf
The Portuguese invasion of the Gulf islands and the east coast paves the way for Arabia to start trading with British, French and Dutch ships.

4 1793: Al Bu Falah tribe settles in Abu Dhabi
The Al Bu Falah and Al Nahayan tribes settle in Abu Dhabi.

5 1833: Al Maktoum tribe arrives in Dubai
Under the leadership of Maktoum bin Buti Al Maktoum, the Al Maktoum tribe settles at the mouth of Dubai Creek.

6 1894: Tax-free trading
Dubai introduces tax exemptions for foreigners. Persians are the first expats.

7 1950s: Discovery of oil
Oil is discovered in Abu Dhabi in 1958 and Dubai in 1966. The fortunes of the cities are immediately transformed.

8 1971: UAE established
The seven emirates become the UAE Federation, with Sheikh Zayed bin Sultan Al Nahyan, ruler of Abu Dhabi, as the new President.

9 2004: Death of Sheikh Zayed
The UAE goes into mourning with the death of its president.

10 2008: Credit crunch
The global financial crisis sends Dubai to the brink of bankruptcy before intervention from Abu Dhabi.

🔟 Art Galleries

1 Folklore Gallery
MAP Q2 ■ Zayed 1st Street, Al Khalidiya, Abu Dhabi ■ 02 666 0361 ■ Open 9am–1pm & 4pm–9pm Sat–Thu

One of the best places to find works of art and craft from across the region, including handmade greeting cards, Turkish bookmarks, prints and handblown glass.

2 Majlis Gallery
MAP K2 ■ Al Musalla roundabout, Al Fahidi neighbourhood, Dubai ■ 04 353 6233 ■ Open 10am–6pm Sat–Thu ■ www.majlisgallery.com

Dubai's oldest commercial art gallery focuses on Arabian and Middle Eastern themed work by local and expat artists. Browse for good prints, ceramics and sculpture (see p18).

The traditional exterior of XVA

5 XVA
MAP K2 ■ Al Fahidi neighbourhood, Dubai ■ 04 353 5383 ■ Open 10am–6pm ■ www.xvagallery.com

A superb contemporary art gallery set in a stylish boutique hotel in a restored traditional house. The idyllic courtyard café is also used as an exhibition space (see p19).

6 Green Art Gallery
MAP C2 ■ Alserkel Ave, Al Quoz, Dubai ■ 04 346 9305 ■ Open 10am–7pm Sat–Thu ■ Closed first two weeks in August ■ www.gagallery.com

This established commercial gallery in Al Quoz displays the work of Emirati and international artists, with a focus on the heritage, cultures and environment of the Middle East. There is a programme of changing exhibitions throughout the year.

Abstact artwork at the Third Line

3 The Third Line
MAP C2 ■ Street 8, Alserkel Ave, Al Quoz 1, Dubai ■ 04 341 1367 ■ Open 10am–7pm Sat–Thu; call ahead ■ www.thethirdline.com

This gallery showcases playful and edgy work by artists from around the Gulf. Displays change every couple of weeks.

4 The Empty Quarter
MAP D6 ■ Building 2, the Gate Village, Dubai ■ 04 323 1210 ■ Open 10am–7pm Sun–Thu ■ www.theemptyquarter.com

This is the UAE's only fine-art photography gallery. It features Middle Eastern and international documentary and creative work.

Kanoo exhibition of Pop Art at Art Space

7 Abu Dhabi Art Hub

MAP U4 ▪ Plot 38, Musaffah, Abu Dhabi ▪ 02 551 5005 ▪ Open 9am–7pm Sat–Thu ▪ www.adah.ae

Focusing on both emerging and established visual artists, this gallery encourages interaction and cross-cultural artistic exchanges between national and international artists.

8 Etihad Modern Art Gallery

MAP Q3 ▪ Al Bateen Area, Villa 15, Huwelat St, Abu Dhabi ▪ 02 621 0145 ▪ Open 10am–10pm Sat–Thu ▪ www. etihadmodernart.com

This contemporary gallery encourages the creation of art with local references, exhibiting work from well-established and upcoming Emirati and international artists.

9 Gallery Isabelle van den Eynde

MAP C2 ▪ Alserkal Ave, Al Quoz, Dubai ▪ 04 323 5052 ▪ Open 10am–7pm Sat–Thu ▪ www.ivde.net

This gallery predominantly represents Middle Eastern artists and favours provocative paintings, photography and mixed media works. Standout shows include Iranian artist Ramin Haerizadeh's photo-manipulation using his own face to recreate themes from Persian theatre.

10 Art Space

MAP D6 ▪ Gate Village, DIFC, Dubai ▪ 04 323 0820 ▪ Open 9am–6pm Sun–Thu

With a mission to nurture local talent, this gallery has hosted great exhibitions by Middle Eastern and Emirati artists. Highlights include Mohammed Kanoo's playful Pop Art.

TOP 10 FESTIVALS AND EVENTS

Abu Dhabi Desert Challenge

1 Dubai Marathon
Jan ▪ www.dubaimarathon.org
An annual marathon race across the city.

2 Dubai World Cup
MAP D3 ▪ Meydan racetrack ▪ Feb–Mar ▪ www.dubaiworldcup.com
The world's richest horse-racing cup.

3 Dubai Tennis Championships
Feb–Mar ▪ www.dubaidutyfreetennischampionships.com
Players battle it out at this tennis event.

4 Dubai Desert Classic
MAP B2 ▪ Mar ▪ www.dubaidesertclassic.com
A renowned golf tournament.

5 Art Dubai
Madinat Arena ▪ Mar ▪ www.artdubai.ae
Dubai's biggest contemporary art fair.

6 Dubai International Jazz Festival
MAP B2 ▪ Dubai Media City ▪ Mar ▪ www.dubaijazzfest.com
Crowds gather for performances by some of the world's biggest jazz names.

7 Abu Dhabi Desert Challenge
Apr ▪ www.abudhabidesertchallenge.com
A 4-day motor rally through the desert.

8 Dubai International Film Festival
MAP C2 ▪ Madinat Jumeirah ▪ Dec ▪ www.dubaifilmfest.com
Glam galas and film screenings take place during this week-long event.

9 Global Village
MAP C3 ▪ Dubailand, Emirates Rd ▪ Dec–Feb ▪ www.globalvillage.ae
A huge fun fair and shopping bazaar celebrating multiculturalism.

10 Dubai Shopping Festival
Citywide ▪ Dec–Feb ▪ www.mydsf.ae
A retail and entertainment extravaganza, with sales, shows and events.

🔟 Resorts in Dubai

1 Al Qasr

Opulent to the last detail, this extravagant hotel looks almost like a Hollywood film set, with sweeping staircases, supersized chandeliers and lavish Arabian styling *(see p113)*. It is also where you will find the romantic Pierchic restaurant *(see p81)*, which offers memorable views of the nearby Burj Al Arab Jumeirah.

Jumeirah Zabeel Saray interior

2 Jumeirah Zabeel Saray

Dubai's fondness for extravagant interior design reaches fever pitch at this extraordinary Palm resort *(see p113)*, with a series of show-stopping restaurants and bars ranging from the stunning Indian-style Amala restaurant *(see p87)* to the futuristic Voda Bar *(see p86)*.

3 Jumeirah Beach Hotel

Dubai's famous wave-shaped resort *(see p113)* is home to the ever-popular Wild Wadi Water Park *(see p78)*. Non-guests also flock to the hotel for its vast selection of restaurants and bars, including the trendy club Mahiki and 360°, a super-cool cocktail bar *(see p81)*.

4 Ritz Carlton

Traditional European design and understated elegance reign supreme at the superior Ritz Carlton *(see p114)*. Savour the hotel's style over a sumptuous afternoon tea at the immaculate Lobby Lounge, sip cocktails in the opulent Library Bar or enjoy a spot of pampering at the hotel's luxury spa.

5 Raffles

All things ancient Egyptian are the order of the day in this pyramid-shaped city hotel *(see p112)*. The lavish foyer, with its huge hieroglyphic columns, is a sight in its own right, while views from the top of the building can be enjoyed during a visit to the trendy Tomo Japanese restaurant or an evening at the glitzy nightclub People by Crystal.

The vast foyer at Raffles

The opulent One&Only Royal Mirage

6 One&Only Royal Mirage

With Moorish-style buildings, Dubai's most romantic hotel is spread out along the beach amidst a forest of palms (see p113). Visit to savour the atmosphere and explore the outstanding restaurants, including Eauzone (see p87) and Tagine (see p87), and relax in the stunning Oriental Spa.

7 Atlantis, The Palm

This towering arch-shaped resort (see p113) at the end of the Palm is one of the city's most famous landmarks and is also home to several leading family attractions, including the Lost Chambers (see p83) and Aquaventure (see p84). Non-guests can also use the beautiful hotel beach.

8 Park Hyatt

A real urban retreat in the heart of the city, the Park Hyatt's serene Moroccan styling and beautiful creekside setting offer a genuine sanctuary for the senses (see p112). The place is best appreciated over a meal at the Thai Kitchen restaurant (see p63) or with a glass of champagne at the waterfront bar The Terrace (see p62).

9 Burj Al Arab Jumeirah

No trip to Dubai is complete without a visit to the most famous building in the city – and perhaps the world. Enjoy a memorable afternoon tea in the dazzlingly decorated atrium or take in stunning views over a cocktail in the sky-high Skyview Bar (see pp24–5).

10 The Palace

A haven of traditional Arabian style amidst the modern developments of Downtown Dubai (see p112). Admire the hotel's sumptuous styling and stunning lakeside setting, and have a meal at the romantic Thiptara restaurant (see p75) or take afternoon tea in the decadent Al Bayt Lounge.

There are numerous attractions for day-trippers at Atlantis, The Palm

ⓂⒶ⓿ Children's Attractions

An exhilarating water slide at the Aquaventure water park

① Magic Planet
MAP E2 ■ Deira City Centre, Dubai ■ 04 295 4333 ■ Open 10am–11pm Sat–Wed, 10am–midnight Thu–Fri ■ Adm for rides ■ www.deiracitycentre.com

An indoor entertainment venue for all the family, with a merry-go-round, bumper cars, pitch and putt golf, and video games for children, and a soft-play area for toddlers.

② Ski Dubai Snow Park
All ski levels and ages can try their hand at skiing or snowboarding on the slopes of the largest indoor snow park in the world. You can also meet the resident penguins during the 40-minute Penguin Encounter, or watch them for free during the March of the Penguins *(see p77)*.

Watching the skiers at Ski Dubai

③ Aquaventure
Sprawled across 17 ha (43 acres) next to the Atlantis resort, this vast water park has plenty to thrill visitors. Travel through rapids, waterfalls and the death-defying Leap of Faith slide *(see p84)*.

④ MOTIONGATE™ Dubai
MAP B2 ■ Sheikh Zayed Rd, Dubai ■ 04 820 0000 ■ Open 11am–8pm Sun–Wed, 11am–10pm Thu–Sat ■ Adm ■ www.dubaiparksandresorts.com

Enjoy rides and shows based on the *Smurfs*, *Kung Fu Panda* and many other movies, at the Middle East's largest Hollywood-inspired theme park.

⑤ IMG Worlds of Adventure
MAP C3 ■ Sheikh Mohammed Bin Zayed Rd, Dubai ■ 04 403 8888 ■ Open 11am–9pm Sun–Wed, 11am–10pm Thu–Sat ■ Adm ■ www.imgworlds.com

This large indoor amusement park is split into four themed zones, including two based on Marvel Comics and Cartoon Network, and the exciting Lost Valley – Dinosaur Adventure.

⑥ Wild Wadi Water Park
Dare to try some of the 30 adrenaline-fuelled watery rides or just float about on a rubber ring along the waterways of this enormous outdoor water park *(see p78)*.

7 Yas Waterworld
Yas Island, Abu Dhabi ▪ 02 414 2000 ▪ Adm ▪ www.yaswaterworld.com
Offering fun-filled adventures for all ages, this Emirati-themed water park features 45 rides, slides and attractions for the whole family.

8 Kidzania
MAP C6 ▪ Dubai Mall, Dubai ▪ Open 10am–10pm (till 11pm Fri–Sat ▪ Adm; under 2s free ▪ www.kidzania.ae
Children take over the world at Kidzania, a miniature city in which kids can dress up in costumes and role-play from a selection of different jobs, including policeman and fireman.

9 Children's City
MAP K3 ▪ Creek Park, Dubai ▪ 04 334 0808 ▪ Open 9am–7pm Sun–Thu, 2–8pm Fri & Sat ▪ Adm; under 2s free ▪ www.childrencity.dm.gov.ae
Housed in a brightly coloured building, this play zone places an emphasis on education. Activities focus on subjects ranging from space exploration to international culture.

The futuristic Sega Republic

10 Sega Republic
MAP C6 ▪ Dubai Mall, Dubai ▪ 04 448 8484 ▪ Open 10am–midnight ▪ Adm ▪ www.segarepublic.com
Inside the Dubai Mall is an enormous amusement arcade and theme park. Pay individually for rides, games and attractions, or buy a combined pass.

TOP 10 PARKS, GARDENS AND BEACHES

Jumeirah Beach Park

1 Creekside Park
A huge botanical park with BBQ areas, a mini golf course and a cable car (see p16).

2 Za'abeel Park
MAP F5–F6 ▪ Sheikh Zayed Rd, Dubai
A technology-themed park with a football field, boating lake and cafés.

3 Al Seef Rd Park
MAP K2 ▪ Dubai
A great place to enjoy the creek action.

4 Jumeirah Beach Park
This park has landscaped play areas and a beach with sunbeds (see p78).

5 Al Mamzar Beach Park
MAP F1 ▪ Al Hamriya, Dubai ▪ 04 296 6201 ▪ Open 8am–10pm; Mon is for women and children (boys under 4) only ▪ Adm
A child-friendly beach park with huge picnic areas, four swimming beaches, a mini train and bikes for hire.

6 Umm Suqeim Beach
MAP C2 ▪ Off Jumeirah Beach Rd, Dubai
This public beach has shallow waters and views of the Burj Al Arab Jumeirah.

7 Safa Park
A huge park with lots to do. Try the trampoline cage for fun (see p77).

8 Mushrif Park
MAP F3 ▪ Al Khawaneej Rd, Dubai ▪ Open 8am–10:30pm Sat–Wed, 8am–11:30pm Thu–Fri ▪ Adm
A desert park with pools, farm animals, a theatre and a botanic garden.

9 Russian Beach
MAP D4 ▪ Jumeirah Rd, Dubai
This lively local beach is popular with Russian expats and tourists.

10 Kite Beach
MAP C2 ▪ Umm Suqeim, behind Wollongong University, Dubai
A popular spot for watersports.

🔟 Outdoor Activities

Skydiving over the Palm Jumeirah

3 Wind Surfing
Great winds make Dubai an ideal wind-surfing destination. Most good beach resorts hire out equipment and also offer wind-surfing lessons. The Westin Mina Seyahi hotel (see p113) is particularly renowned for its facilities.

4 Fishing
Join an organized fishing trip where equipment is provided. Cook your fish on board or charter your own boat. Le Meridien Mina Seyahi Resort in Dubai (see p113) and the Beach Rotana in Abu Dhabi (see p116) offer great fishing trips.

1 Skydiving
Skydive Dubai: MAP B1; Al Sufouh Rd, Dubai; 04 377 8888; www.skydivedubai.ae
For the ultimate Dubai high, strap yourself into a parachute and dive into the city. Skydive Dubai arrange tandem jumps over the Palm Jumeirah, and run a training school in the desert.

5 Motor Racing
Dubai Autodrome Kart-drome: Emirates Rd, Dubai; MAP B3; 04 367 8700; www.dubaiautodrome.com
Adrenaline-junkies can burn rubber driving pro-karts at the Dubai Autodrome. The Formula 1 standard racing circuit has 17 hair-raising turns. Book ahead for lessons at the excellent driving school.

2 Scuba Diving
Emirates Diving Association: MAP K1; Heritage Village and Diving Village, Al Shindagha; 04 393 9390; www.emiratesdiving.com
A popular local activity, the Emirates Diving Association offers information on diving in Dubai, Abu Dhabi and some of the East Coast towns.

Racing car, the Autodrome

6 Hot-air Ballooning
Getting a bird's-eye-view of the desert from a hot-air balloon is simply sublime. Only by floating way above the dunes can you fully appreciate the waves of sand and patterns of light and shadow crafted by the ridges that are impossible to see from the ground (see p32).

A hot-air balloon floating over the desert landscape

7 Wakeboarding

Hiltonia Beach Club: MAP Q2; Corniche Road West; Abu Dhabi; 02 692 4205; www3.hilton.com

Try your hand at some wakeboarding tricks on the Arabian Gulf sea. If you're a first-timer, the best place to learn is at a resort. Le Meridien Mina Seyahi Resort in Dubai (see p113) and the Hiltonia Beach Club in Abu Dhabi offer great lessons.

8 Golfing

Dubai Golf: www.dubaigolf.com

Both Dubai and Abu Dhabi are awash with world-beating courses. Several international competitions take place every year, including the Dubai Desert Classic at the city's largest course, the Emirates Golf Club.

Golfing in front of the Dubai skyline

9 Kite Surfing

Kite Beach: MAP C2; Jumeirah Beach, Dubai ▪ North Kites: 04 394 1258, www.northkites.com

Join the local kite surfers on Dubai's Kite Beach. You can hire or buy equipment from North Kites, who will help connect you with instructors.

10 Horseriding

Emirates Equestrian Centre: MAP D3; 050 558 7656 ▪ Abu Dhabi Equestrian Club: Al Ain, 02 445 5500

With its world-class equestrian centre, Dubai is the Middle East's undisputed horseriding capital. There is also a top equestrian centre in Abu Dhabi, which offers riding lessons.

TOP 10 SPECTATOR SPORTS

Runner in the Dubai Marathon

1 Dubai World Cup
Dress up for the world's richest horse race with a $6 million prize (see p39).

2 Dubai Desert Classic
Watch the world's best golfers compete in this 4-day tournament (see p39).

3 Dubai Tennis Championships
See the big guns of world tennis serve action at Dubai Tennis Stadium (see p39).

4 Dubai Rugby Sevens
Nov ▪ www.dubairugby7s.com
The first leg of the Sevens World Tour is loved by rugby fans all over the world.

5 Camel Racing
Al Wathba Camel Track, 45 km (30 miles) east of Abu Dhabi
▪ Oct–Mar Thu–Fri
Watch Emiratis drive their 4WDs around the track beside their camels.

6 F1 Grand Prix
Dates vary ▪ www.yasmarinacircuit.com
Since 2009, Abu Dhabi has hosted a race at the Yas Marina circuit.

7 UAE Football
Winter weekday nights ▪ www.proleague.ae
The choreographed dances and songs by the fans are just as riveting as the play on the field at this popular event.

8 Powerboat Racing
Dec ▪ www.f1h2o.com
Watch the lightweight catamarans in action at this exciting race.

9 Dubai Marathon
Runners from all around the world compete on the city streets (see p39).

10 Abu Dhabi Desert Challenge
Bikes, 4WDs and even trucks take part in this international cross-country rally through the desert (see p39).

🔟 Restaurants

1 Mezlai
MAP N1 ▪ Emirates Palace, Dubai ▪ 02 690 7999 ▪ Open 1–10:30pm ▪ DDD

This innovative restaurant features authentic Emirati cuisine in a lavish setting. Guests are given five-star treatment and can choose from a selection of local dishes, including fire-grilled seafood, Gulf-style biryanis and creamy desserts.

The lavish dining room at Mezlai

2 Buddha Bar
A cavernous, dimly-lit restaurant overseen by an enormous Buddha, this is Dubai's most spec-tacular piece of culinary theatre. Food focuses on Pan-Asian cuisine, including an excellent selection of Japanese dishes (see p87).

3 Bord Eau
French fine dining is the theme at this upmarket restaurant housed in Abu Dhabi's Shangri-La Hotel. Opt for the blind-tasting menu, and choose between a seat in the beautiful old-world dining room or on the terrace outside (see p101).

4 Qbara
MAP E2 ▪ Wafi City (adjacent to Raffles Hotel), Dubai ▪ 04 709 2500 ▪ Open 6pm–1am ▪ DDD

There's a distinct hint of Arabian magic in this very chic restaurant, with its intimate, dimly-lit interior and star-like illuminations twinkling overhead. Arabia dominates the menu, too, with mouthwatering mezze and inventive mains.

5 Anise
Modelled on the eight points of the star anise, this charming eatery offers eight cooking stations. Diners can watch as the chefs create their meal with flair and passion. It also has a beautiful terrace that boasts views over the Dubai Creek (see p63).

6 Eauzone
Located in the One&Only Royal Mirage (see p113), this is one of Dubai's most romantic res-taurants. Visit after dark and dine at tables in miniature Arabian tents set between floodlit pools. The food features top-quality Pan-Asian cuisine including some traditional classics and delicious contemporary fusion creations (see p87).

Eauzone, set beside a floodlit pool

A table setting at Indego by Vineet

7 Indego by Vineet

Vineet Bhatia, India's first Michelin-starred chef, showcases his unique talents at this stylish restaurant. It offers a mix of traditional Indian favourites alongside more unusual contemporary creations, blending European and subcontinental influences (see p87).

8 Hoi An

The spirit of colonial-era French Indochina lives on at these beautiful wood-panelled restaurants, located in the Shangri-La Hotel in both Dubai and Abu Dhabi. The menu offers delicious and innovative Vietnamese–French cuisine (see p75 & p101).

9 Rhodes Twenty10

The brainchild of UK celebrity chef Gary Rhodes, this unpretentious and affordable restaurant serves up Rhodes' signature reworkings of traditional British classics alongside a selection of more Middle Eastern-influenced creations (see p87).

10 Pai Thai

Approached by *abra* (water taxi), this waterfront restaurant offers one of Dubai's most romantic dining experiences. The stunning setting is perfectly complemented by the fresh and authentic Thai food. Expect crisply flavoured curries (see p81).

TOP 10 MIDDLE EASTERN RESTAURANTS

1 Tagine
An exquisitely decorated restaurant serving fine Moroccan cuisine (see p87).

2 Arabian Tea House Café
Affordable Arabian fare is served in a pretty courtyard garden (see p69).

3 Zahr el Laymoun
MAP B6 ▪ Souk Al Bahar, Dubai ▪ 04 448 6060 ▪ Open 10am–midnight ▪ www.zahrellaymoun.com ▪ DD
Enjoy good Lebanese cuisine at this place overlooking the Dubai Fountain.

4 Shabestan
MAP L2 ▪ Radisson Blu Hotel, Dubai Creek ▪ 04 205 7333 ▪ Open 12:30–3:30pm & 7:30–11:30pm ▪ DDD
Expect quality Iranian cuisine and creek views at this hotel restaurant.

5 Awtar
MAP E2 ▪ Grand Hyatt Dubai, Dubai ▪ 04 317 2222 ▪ Open 7:30pm–3am Sun–Fri ▪ DDD
This place offers good Lebanese food with regular bellydancing performances.

6 Al Nafoorah
Top-quality Lebanese cuisine is served in a sedate setting (see p75).

7 Almaz by Momo
A Moroccan café owned by restaurateur Mourad "Momo" Mazouz (see p81).

8 Bastakiah Nights
A lovely courtyard restaurant in a beautiful old Al Fahidi mansion (see p19).

9 Atayeb
MAP W4 ▪ Yas Viceroy, Abu Dhabi ▪ 02 656 0600 ▪ Open 7pm–1am Sun–Fri ▪ DD
Offers an iconic view. Dishes include Emirati fare.

10 Lebanese Flower
Abu Dhabi residents flock to this excellent Lebanese restaurant (see p95).

Arabian Tea House Café

For a key to restaurant price ranges see p63

🔟 Best Bars in Dubai

Vivid blue and green decor at the popular Skyview Bar

① Skyview Bar

Jutting out from the top of the Burj Al Arab Jumeirah, this is one of Dubai's ultimate places for a drink. Sweeping views up and down the coast are accompanied by a superior list of cocktails, wines and other drinks. Advance booking is required *(see p24)*.

② The Rooftop

It is easy to fall in love with the magical look and feel of this atmospheric Moroccan-style rooftop bar, with its Arabesque lanterns and Oriental lounge music *(see p86)*.

Moroccan styling at the Rooftop

③ Vault

At the top of the JW Marriott Marquis, Vault is another head-in-the-clouds bar with amazing views across Dubai. Chic decor and cocktails attract a monied crowd *(see p74)*.

④ Bar 44

Prop yourself up at the swanky circular bar or sink into a plush chair at this swish cocktail bar on level 44 (hence the name) of the Grosvenor House hotel. It attracts a regular sophisticated local set as well as visiting businesspeople out to impress colleagues with spectacular views over Dubai Marina *(see p86)*.

⑤ Up on the Tenth

MAP L2 ▪ Radisson Blue, Bani Yas Rd, Dubai ▪ 04 205 7033 ▪ Open 6:30pm–3am

Hidden away in Deira's Radisson Blu hotel, Up on the Tenth is one of the city's better-kept secrets. The bar itself is smart but unremarkable, but the stunning view over the creek is perhaps the best in the whole of the old city. Arrive early to bag a seat by the window and then while away the evening listening to the bar's nightly jazz performances.

⑥ Asia Asia

Embark on a journey from Asia Minor through to the Far East at this extravagant restaurant. The exciting menu takes inspiration from the ancient Spice Route *(see p74)*.

7 The Terrace
Reclining on one of the low sofas at this bar and listening to the water lapping at the boats on Dubai Creek is about as relaxing as life gets. Add some oysters, champagne and caviar to the equation and you're bound to have a sublime experience. The Terrace prides itself on its extensive vodka menu (see p62).

8 At.mosphere
On the 122nd floor of the Burj Khalifa, At.mosphere is the world's highest bar, offering jaw-dropping views in swanky surroundings. Most people come to eat in the attached restaurant, but you can also book yourself in for a drink. Advance reservations are required (see p75).

9 Bahri Bar
You'll be impressed with the enchanting old-Arabian details and sumptuous interiors of the colonial-styled bar at the Mina A'Salam hotel. Nurse a drink on the veranda and take in the mesmerizing view of the Burj Al Arab Jumeirah (see p81).

Views from the veranda, Bahri Bar

10 360°
Perched amidst the waves at the end of a breakwater, 360° has one of the very best views in Dubai, with the Burj Al Arab Jumeirah and Jumeirah Beach Hotel rising to either side. Chill-out music and DJs attract a cool crowd, and it's a good place to lounge over a sheesha (see p81).

TOP 10 SHEESHA SPOTS

Shimmers, located on the beach

1 The Courtyard
MAP B1 = One&Only Royal Mirage Hotel, Jumeirah, Dubai = 04 399 9999 = Open 6am–1pm
A great selection of aromatic tobacco blends in a cushion-strewn courtyard.

2 Kan Zaman
Smoke under the stars at this authentic Arabic café by the creek (see p69).

3 Shimmers
MAP C2 = Madinat Jumeirah, Dubai = 04 432 3232 = Open noon–1pm
Sheesha at a deluxe beach shack.

4 Shakespeare & Co
MAP D4 = The Village Mall, Dubai = 04 344 6228 = Open 8am–1am
A French Baroque-style patisserie by day, and a sheesha bar at night.

5 Souk Madinat Jumeirah
The central plaza is a breezy, magical spot to smoke sheesha (see p80).

6 QDs
Expats love this great smoking spot overlooking the creek (see p62).

7 Barouk
MAP E5 = Crowne Plaza, Yas Island, Abu Dhabi = 02 656 3000
A lebanese eatery with sheesha terrace.

8 Khan Murjan
MAP E2 = Wafi City, Dubai = 04 327 9795 = Open 10am–12:30am
The grandeur of a 14th- century souk, in the heart of Modern Dubai.

9 Al Hakawati Café
MAP B2 = Dubai Marina, Jumeirah, Dubai = 04 288 8396 = Open 10am–1am
Smoke amongst towering skyscrapers.

10 Special Sheesha Café
Branches on Abu Dhabi Corniche = Open 24 hours
Join the locals at these simple cafés.

🔟 Shopping Malls and Souks

Textiles for sale, Souk Al Bahar

1 Souk Al Bahar
Just over the waterway from the Dubai Mall is this more Arabic-themed affair featuring an array of boutique and antique shops. There is also an excellent selection of eateries and bars *(see p72)*.

2 Mall of the Emirates
Over 520 stores, including a swish Harvey Nichols, make this the city's most sumptuous mall. If you're in a rush, use the mall's website to create an itinerary identifying the most direct route to the shops you wish to visit *(see p79)*.

3 Marina Mall (Dubai)
MAP P1 ▪ Exit 32 off Sheikh Zayed Rd ▪ 04 436 1020 ▪ Open 10am–10pm Sat–Wed, 10am–midnight Thu–Fri
This sleek, modern mall on the marina waterfront is bursting with upmarket designer boutiques set around a huge circular atrium.

4 Dubai Festival City
MAP E3 ▪ Al Rebat St, Dubai ▪ 800 332 22 ▪ Open 10am–10pm Sun–Wed, 10am–midnight Thu–Sat
This waterfront development offers a French Riviera-style marina, excellent shopping and alfresco dining. It has more than 400 shops, including a huge Marks & Spencer and an IKEA.

5 Marina Mall (Abu Dhabi)
With over 300 shops, expect big name brands, exclusive stores such as Rolex and Tiffany & Co, and traditional Arabian perfume, sweets and clothes shops. The excellent cafés include Hediard from Paris *(see p91)*.

6 Wafi City
This quirky mall is adorned with pharaonic statues, miniature pyramids and assorted hieroglyphics. Shops include some excellent independent fashion boutiques and the Wafi Gourmet deli *(see p68)*.

Mall of the Emirates, crowned by an impressive glass dome

Shopping Malls and Souks « 51

7 Abu Dhabi Mall

Generally considered to be Abu Dhabi's smartest mall, this place boasts a huge array of shops arranged over three floors. You can find everything from designer fashion through to electronics and home furnishings (see p94).

8 Ibn Battuta Mall

As soon as you see the six themed shopping zones and food courts within this mall, you won't regret your long drive out to Emirates Hills. The decor for each area is inspired by the countries that Arabia's own Marco Polo, Ibn Battuta, travelled to: Tunisia, Egypt, Persia, India, Andalucia and China. There is also a 21-screen cinema (see p83).

Ibn Battuta's exotic interior

9 The Galleria

One of Abu Dhabi's new consumer additions, the Galleria houses boutique stores owned by world-class luxury brands. It is set across three floors (see p94).

10 The Dubai Mall

Next to the world's biggest tower sits the world's largest shopping mall. This monument to consumerism houses over 1,000 stores, not to mention an ice rink, an aquarium, and a vast cinema and entertainment complex. The mall also boasts over 150 food outlets, offering everything from fine dining to casual eateries. For Emiratis, the Dubai Mall is as much about socializing as shopping (see p73).

TOP 10 THINGS TO BUY

A selection of traditional *khanjars*

1 Gold and gems
Gold prices in Dubai are amongst the cheapest found anywhere in the world, while precious stones (diamonds in particular) are also very keenly priced.

2 Carpets
Numerous shops across the UAE sell opulent Persian carpets at prices significantly lower than you would pay back home. Make sure you bargain hard.

3 Perfume
Concoct your own scent from Arabian oils *(attar)* in a local perfume shop.

4 Arabian handicrafts
Collectible local handicrafts include traditional Arabian-style coffeepots, traditional *khanjars* (daggers) and miniature carved wooden boxes.

5 Fun souvenirs
Mosque-shaped alarm clocks, cuddly camels and Burj Khalifa paperweights all make enjoyable mementos.

6 Designer fakes
Branded bags, watches and other replica designer accessories are widely available in Karama and Deira.

7 Bedouin jewellery
Chunky antique silver bangles, necklaces and rings make unusual but affordable souvenirs.

8 Music
Stock up on a selection of recordings of Middle Eastern music, from more traditional Emirati singers to Egyptian and Lebanese pop megastars.

9 Aladdin slippers
Dress like Aladdin in a pair of curly-toed Arabian slippers.

10 Electronics
Keen competition keeps prices low for mobiles, laptops and tablets.

🔟 Dubai and Abu Dhabi for Free

The striking white façade of Sheikh Zayed Mosque, a principal religious site

1 Movies Under the Stars
MAP E2 ■ Wafi City,
Oud Metha Rd, Dubai ■ 04 324 4100
■ www.pyramidsrestaurantsatwafi.com
Grab a beanbag and settle down to enjoy a free open-air film-screening every Sunday (8:30pm) from October to May in the pretty rooftop garden above the Wafi City complex (see p68).

2 Free Museums
Museum admission rarely costs more than a few dirhams, but some places – including Dubai's Coffee Museum (see p18), the Traditional Architecture Museum (see p67), Heritage House (see p59), Al-Ahmadiya School (see p59) and the Abu Dhabi Heritage Village (see p92) – are completely free.

Exhibits at the Coffee Museum

3 Sheikh Zayed Mosque
Abu Dhabi's single biggest tourist attraction is absolutely free to enter – and there are even gratis guided tours (see pp28–9).

4 Dubai Trolley
Free rides around Downtown Dubai are available every evening outside summer (5pm–1am daily) aboard the cute Dubai Trolley, an antique-style trolley-tram running on tracks alongside Mohammed bin Rashid Boulevard. Sit upstairs for cooling breezes and the best views.

5 Art for Free
Dubai's many art galleries offer endless scope for seeing the work of leading Middle Eastern and other artists at zero cost – unless you want to take a piece home (see pp38–9).

6 Amazing Malls
Some of Dubai's malls are virtual tourist attractions in their own right. Top picks include the extravagantly decorated Ibn Battuta Mall (see p83) and the upscale Mall of the Emirates (see p79), which has surreal views of the snow-clad slopes of Ski Dubai, complete with the occasional penguin (see p77).

⑦ Waterside Walks

The breezy walks along the Bur Dubai side (south) of the creek (see pp16–17) in Dubai and along the Abu Dhabi Corniche (see p90) are spectacular. You'll see some of the best sights in these intriguing cities and it won't cost you a penny.

⑧ Free Beaches

The huge sandy beach at the Dubai Marina (see p84) is a popular local destination, with plenty of facilities available, including water sports. In Abu Dhabi, there's a fine stretch of free soft white sand and clear blue sea fringing the city's beautiful Corniche (see p90).

⑨ Ras Al Khor Wildlife Sanctuary

Settle into a hide and watch colourful flocks of bright pink flamingos and other birds framed against a surreal backdrop of skyscrapers. It is free to use the hides but groups of 10 or more require a permit (see p72).

Ras Al Khor Wildlife Sanctuary

⑩ Dubai Fountain

Dubai's record-breaking choreographed fountain, set in the middle of Burj Khalifa Lake, can be enjoyed for free every evening and most afternoons from any part of the broad pedestrianized walkway running around the lake. This must-see experience offers close-up views of the dancing jets and watery swirls as they rise up, accompanied by dramatic music (see p71).

TOP 10 MONEY-SAVING TIPS

Dubai's Gold Souk

1 Purchase a Nol Card to make the most of Dubai's excellent metro. The card can also be used on buses, water buses and trams (www.nol.ae)

2 The old city is absolutely crammed full of Indian curry houses and *shawarma* cafés offering excellent food at great bargain prices.

3 While summer is best avoided due to the ferocious heat, hotel rates often plunge between May and September.

4 Check online or with travel agents for combined hotel-plus-flight packages rather than booking travel and accommodation separately.

5 Bringing cash from home and changing it locally will often work out cheaper than using plastic, which can mean having to pay hefty credit card and ATM fees.

6 Many bars have regular midweek "ladies' nights", offering free drinks to members of the fairer sex.

7 Take advantage of the regular happy hours (generally from 6pm to 8pm daily). Offers during this time can massively reduce the cost of a drink.

8 Don't be afraid of haggling over prices in the old city souks, especially in Dubai's Gold Souk (see p26).

9 If you want designer brands without the Hollywood price tag, shops in Karama Souk (see p27) offer a vast array of convincing fakes at affordable prices. Have an idea of how much you want to pay and bargain hard.

10 Dubai's many festivals (see p39) often include activities, events and entertainment either for free or at very discounted prices.

 Excursions and Tours

3 Hatta

105 km (65 miles) from Dubai ■ **Heritage Village: open 8am–7:30pm Sat–Thu, 3–9pm Fri**

Visit the Heritage Village at this serene oasis town. A drive into the mountains from here leads to the clear Hatta Rock Pools, a fantastically beautiful spot for swimming.

4 Al Ain

160 km (99 miles) from Dubai ■ **Al Ain Palace Museum: 03 751 7755** ■ **Jahili Fort: next to Al Ain Rotana Hotel** ■ **Al Ain Camel Souk: Al Ain-Buraimi border**

Known as Garden City, this green emirate is home to the Al Ain Palace Museum. Also here are the Al Ain Livestock Souk and the Jahili Fort.

1 Wonder Bus Tour

04 359 5656 ■ **www.wonderbusdubai.net**

This one-hour tour starts with a drive down to Shindagha in Bur Dubai, at which point the vehicle plunges into the creek for a cruise through the old city before returning to land.

2 Liwa

300 km (186 miles) from Abu Dhabi

Liwa's high golden dunes are almost devoid of vegetation yet close by are flourishing date-producing farms – an awesome spectacle *(see p32)*.

Liwa's sandswept roads

Pot, Heritage Museum, Sharjah

5 Sharjah

10 km (6 miles) from Dubai ■ **Sharjah Art Museum: 06 568 8222** ■ **Heritage Museum: 06 569 3999** ■ **Archaeological Museum: 06 566 5466**

The Sharjah Art Museum, the Heritage Museum and the Archaeological Museum are must-see sights. The souks here are also very good for shopping.

Rugged mountain scenery on the Musandam Peninsula

6 Musandam Peninsula

193 km (120 miles) from Dubai ■ Khasab Travel & Tours: www.khasabtours.com ■ Visa available at Oman entry point

With amazing mountain cliffs and a coastline of inlets and fjords, this northerly enclave is part of Oman. Enjoy *dhow* day-trips into the fjords.

7 Fujairah

130 km (81 miles) from Dubai

Fujairah has a coastline of coral reefs and hillsides with forts and watchtowers. The Fujairah Fort is the oldest in the UAE, dating to 1670.

8 The Yellow Boats

www.theyellowboats.com

For the best views of the modern city, head out on the water with the Yellow Boats. Tours run up and down the coast starting from Dubai Marina, offering superlative views of the Marina skyscrapers, Atlantis and the Palm, and the Burj Al Arab Jumeirah.

9 Bidiya

38 km (24 miles) north of Fujairah ■ Visit outside of prayer times, accompanied by a mosque guide

This tiny fishing village is home to the oldest mosque in the UAE, dating back to 1446. Made from mud brick, stone and gypsum, it is now restored, with its four small domes held up by a massive central pillar.

Bidiya's 15th-century mosque

10 Al Fahidi Walking Tour

Tours: Tue, Thu, Sat & Sun

Explore Dubai's historic and atmospheric Al Fahidi (Bastakiya) district with an expert guide from the Sheikh Mohammed Centre for Cultural Understanding *(see p18)*. The 90-minute morning tours also include a rare chance to see inside the neighbouring Diwan Mosque and are followed by a Q & A session.

Dubai and Abu Dhabi Area by Area

Towering skyscrapers lining the spectacular man-made Dubai Marina

TOP 10 Deira

Gold Souk goods

The term Deira is used to describe the bustling commercial area north of the creek. Deira is the source of Dubai's trading roots and it is around the creek that you really get a sense of this. There is a telling contrast between the sight of the old wooden *dhows* moored at the wharfside and the glass façades of the sleek skyscrapers that surround them. Much of the *dhow* cargo is destined for the souks and shopping districts of buzzy Deira. As a result, the narrow streets here boast some of Dubai's most atmospheric souks, including the Gold Souk, Spice Souk and Deira Covered Souk. A major preservation effort by Dubai Municipality means that this area offers some architectural gems like the Al-Ahmadiya School and the Heritage House.

DEIRA

- ① **Top 10 Sights**
  see pp59–61
- ① **Restaurants**
  see p63
- ① **Cafés and Bars**
  see p62

0 metres 250
0 yards 250

0 metres 1000
0 yards 1000

Courtyard at Heritage House

1 Heritage House
MAP K1 ■ Al Khor St ■ 04 226 0286 ■ Open 8am–8:30pm Sat–Thu, 2–8:30pm Fri

This beautifully restored airy courtyard house dates back to the 1890s. Unusually, this 10-room building does not have a windtower, but the upper floor is designed with open doors and windows to draw in the creek breezes. Now a museum giving an insight into Emirati history (with dioramas and touch screens), you can explore the different rooms, all in 19th-century furnishings.

2 Al-Ahmadiya School
MAP K1 ■ Al Khor St ■ 04 226 0286 ■ Open 8am–7:30pm Sat–Thu, 2:30–7:30pm Fri

Dubai's first school, opened in 1912, was founded by a philanthropist pearl merchant. Maths, the Holy Koran and Arabic calligraphy were taught and the pupils (all male) sat on palm mats. Many such schools were located in Emirati coastal cities with the support of leading merchants and sheikhs, who subsidised the education. This school closed in 1963. Now a museum, it offers a great educational insight into the past and is worth visiting just for its sheer architectural grace.

3 Food Souk
The sights and smells of a traditional food market provide an enthralling insight into the shopping and eating habits of the locals. On the north side of Deira, this large warehouse-like complex is the old city's major source of fresh food. The colourful fruit and vegetable selection has dozens of stalls piled high with produce, as well as a section specializing in dates from the local area. The gory meat section is for dedicated carnivores only, but the salty-smelling fish section is well worth exploring, with ocean-fresh prawns, hammour and sharks laid out on display (see p27).

4 National Bank of Dubai
MAP L1 ■ Baniyas Rd

Another architectural achievement is the building housing the National Bank of Dubai – one of the city's first iconic buildings. Built in the mid-1990s by Carlos Ott, architect of the Opéra de la Bastille in Paris, it is inspired by the *dhow*. Its curved curtain glass wall symbolizes the billowing sail. The base of the building is clad in green glass, representing water, and its roof is cast in aluminium (denoting the hull of the boat). It is most striking at sunset, when the mirror reflects its gold and silver lights.

National Bank of Dubai's stunning façade

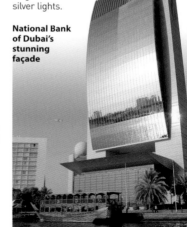

The beautifully manicured greens of the Dubai Creek Golf and Yacht Club

5 Dubai Creek Golf and Yacht Club

MAP E2 ■ Garhoud ■ 04 295 6000

This soaring white building, inspired by the sails of a *dhow* and sitting amidst rolling greens, is a city land-mark, visible from both Maktoum and Garhoud bridges. Opened in January 1993, the world-class golf course here is the centrepiece of a sprawling leisure complex that also incorporates a 115-berth marina. The separate yacht club incorporates the Aquarium, an excellent seafood restaurant, as well as one of Dubai's most popular alfresco eateries, the Boardwalk *(see p63)*, which sits on stilts and offers a spectacular view of the creek, especially at night when the illuminated *dhows* pass by.

6 Perfume Souk

Immediately east of the Gold Souk, Sikkat al Khail Rd is home to an array of shops popularly known

Exotic spices at the Spice Souk

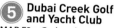

as the Perfume Souk – although there's no actual souk building. Dozens of small shops line the street, selling a mix of international brands and local perfumes. The best are made using the aromatic oud (derived from aloe wood) and come in ornate cut-glass bottles. Most shops also allow you to create your own scents from their selection of perfume oils *(see p27)*.

DEIRA HISTORY

Liberal trade policies are behind the development of Deira, which, by the early 20th century, had become the largest souk on the Arabian coast. It was a haven for merchants who left Lingah, on the Persian coast, after high customs were introduced there in 1902. They continued to trade with Lingah, as do many of the *dhows* in the creek.

7 Spice Souk

Moody and atmospheric, the Spice Souk is a sensory trip into the past, where you can wander through a maze of narrow alleyways of shops piled high with aromatic spices. You'll find sacks of cinnamon sticks, frankincense, cumin, coriander seed and oud. Some great souvenir buys include frankincense (sold with a charcoal burner), henna kits (for hand and body decoration), saffron and fragrant rose water *(see p27)*.

8 Gold Souk

You are unlikely to have ever seen so much gleaming gold as in Dubai's historic Gold Souk. The souk is still dominated by Indian and Iranian craftsmen and traders, as it has been for close on a century. It has been restored with a traditional Arabic arcade and an arching wooden roof. You'll find jewellery in both Arabic and western styles *(see p26)*.

9 Deira Covered Souk

This is where you get a real taste of the melting pot of cultures that is Dubai. The souk is frequented by both Emiratis and expats, and sells everything from bright Indian clothing to colourful kitchenware. There are even household appliances and pirated CDs. It is a fascinating area to wander around *(see p26)*.

Colourful textiles, Deira Covered Souk

10 Dhow Wharfage
MAP L1 ■ Baniyas Rd

A walk along the wharfside beside Baniyas Road allows you to get up close to the painted wooden *dhows*, the traditional Arabian sailing vessels moored here. These ships still trade around the Gulf. Their cargo these days is tyres, refrigerators, air conditioners, electronics – just about any modern item. Moored five or six abreast, these *dhows* have sailed to trade with Dubai from places such as Pakistan and Sudan since the 1830s.

A STROLL THROUGH THE SOUKS

▶ **AFTERNOON**

Aim to start this walk around 4:30pm, when the souk shops re-open after prayers and temperatures are cooler. Start with an *abra* crossing *(see pp16-17)* from the Bur Dubai Abra Station. You can disembark at Deira Old Souk Abra Station. Take the underpass beneath Baniyas Road to emerge at the **Spice Souk** entrance. Enjoy a browse among the fragrant alleyways here. Leave the Spice Souk at Al-Abra St, turn right along Al-Ras St, which leads into Sikkat Al-Khail St. Ahead you will see the latticed entrance to the **Gold Souk**, with its colonnaded interior. There are more than 300 jewellery shops to explore (most accept credit cards).

Wander into the narrow alleyways off the main thoroughfare and enjoy a traditional cup of tea at one of the small cafés.

Exit at the Gold Souk and continue along Sikkat Al-Khail St to the tiny **Perfume Souk**. The shop windows here are a treasure trove of bottles filled with heady Arabian scents, incense and oud.

EVENING

Continue along Sikkat Al-Khail St and enjoy an evening snack at **Ashwaq Cafeteria** *(04 226 1164)*, a down-to-earth café with outdoor tables, serving shwarmas. Next, return to the creek to admire the **Dhow Wharfage**. For a relaxed ending to the day, drop in at Dubai Creek and Yacht Club's **QDs** *(see p62)* and chill out with a cocktail.

See map on p58

Cafés and Bars

1 YUM!
MAP L2 ■ Radisson Blu Hotel ■ 04 222 7171 ■ Open noon–11:30pm ■ D

"Live Fast: East Fast" is this noodle kitchen's motto. Inspired by different Far Eastern cuisines, it makes for a fun pit stop for lunch or a quick dinner.

2 Aroos Damascus
MAP L3 ■ Al Muraqqabat Rd ■ 04 221 9825 ■ Open 6am–3am ■ D

One of the city's best cheap Middle Eastern cafés, with a menu featuring mezze, grills and fish, all beautifully cooked. Try to get a table on the terrace.

3 Creekside
MAP K3 ■ Sheraton Dubai Creek ■ 04 207 1750 ■ Open 6:30–11pm ■ DD

Savour the freshest of fish, expertly prepared Japanese-style, and enjoy the lovely views of the creek.

The Terrace, overlooking the creek

4 The Terrace
MAP E2 ■ Park Hyatt Hotel, Dubai Creek Golf Club ■ 04 602 1814 ■ Open 11am–2am

Made for alfresco drinking and set on the marina front, the Terrace features the Raw Bar, offering a selection of caviar, oysters, prawns and salmon accompanied by a variety of premium vodkas *(see p49)*.

5 QDs
MAP K6 ■ Dubai Creek and Yacht Club ■ 04 295 6000 ■ Open 5pm–2am

Lounge with a sundowner at this creekside wooden-decked terrace bar or enjoy a sheesha at the *majlis* area while the live band plays.

6 Paul
MAP E2 ■ Deira City Centre ■ 04 295 8404 ■ Open 8am–midnight ■ DD

This bustling French brasserie chain has taken the city by storm over the past few years. It serves an excellent array of open sandwiches, salads, and delicious eggs Benedict.

7 Automatic
MAP L3 ■ Al Rigga St ■ 04 294 8333 ■ Open 10am–1am Sat–Wed, 10am–3am Thu & Fri ■ D

This local Lebanese chain is a Dubai institution, with fresh food, great prices and friendly staff. There are a number of branches across the city.

8 Irish Village
MAP E2 ■ Garhoud ■ 04 282 4750 ■ Open 11am–1am Sat–Wed, 11am–2am Thu & Fri

Throw back a pint or two and tuck into some fish and chips in Guinness batter at this Irish-style pub. Find yourself a spot on the outdoor bench seating surrounded by greenery.

9 Belgian Beer Café
MAP E3 ■ Crown Plaza, Dubai Festival City ■ 04 701 1127 ■ Open noon–2am ■ DD

A favourite among expats, the BBC, as it is affectionately known, offers a wide range of Belgian speciality ales and traditional dishes.

10 Eclipse Champagne Bar
MAP E3 ■ InterContinental, Dubai Festival City ■ 04 701 1111 ■ Open 6pm–2am Sat–Wed, 6pm–3am Thu & Fri

This cosy cocktail bar has a real wow factor thanks to its views over Dubai Creek and Sheikh Zayed Road.

Restaurants

1 The China Club
MAP L2 ■ Radisson Blu Hotel
■ 04 222 7171 ■ Open 12:30–3pm &
7:30–11pm daily ■ DD

This elegant restaurant has striking oriental decor and an extensive menu of dim sum and Chinese classics.

The stylish interior of the China Club

2 Table 9
MAP L3 ■ Hilton Dubai
Creek, Baniyas St ■ 04 212 7551
■ Open 6:30pm–midnight ■ DDD

Set up by two British expats, this fine-dining destination is a Dubai favourite. Gastronomic surprises are served in a subtle, upmarket setting.

3 Thai Kitchen
MAP E2 ■ Park Hyatt Hotel,
Dubai Creek Golf Club ■ 04 602 1814
■ Open 7pm–midnight Sat–Thu,
12:30–4pm & 7pm–midnight Fri ■ DD

Thai delicacies are served from live cooking areas. The tasting portions allow you to sample a range of dishes.

4 Blue Elephant
MAP E2 ■ Al Bustan Rotana Hotel,
Al Garhoud Road ■ 04 282 0000 ■ Open
noon–3:30pm & 7pm–midnight ■ DD

A must-visit for the Thai decor, delicious food and warm service.

5 The Bombay
MAP L2 ■ Marco Polo Hotel
■ 04 272 0000 ■ Open 12:30–3pm &
7:30pm–2am ■ DD

This restaurant is considered to be one of the best curry houses in town.

PRICE CATEGORIES

For a three-course meal for one with half a bottle of wine (or equivalent meal), taxes and extra charges.

D Under AED 100 DD AED 100–400
DDD Over AED 400

6 Glasshouse Mediterranean Brasserie
MAP L3 ■ Hilton Dubai Creek, Baniyas
St ■ 04 227 1111 ■ Open
7am–10:30pm ■ DD

A chic, glass-enclosed casual restaurant that serves comfort-food classics. It is the perfect place for a light lunch or an informal dinner.

7 Traiteur
MAP E2 ■ Park Hyatt Hotel,
Dubai Creek Golf Club ■ 04 602 1814
■ Open 6pm–midnight daily & 12:30–
4pm Fri ■ DDD

Enjoy classic European cuisine and admire the chic, modern decor here.

8 Boardwalk
MAP E2 ■ Dubai Creek Golf
Club ■ 04 295 6000 ■ Open 8am–
midnight ■ DD

This restaurant is built on a wooden veranda over the creek, with stunning views, especially by night. The menu is varied, with light Mediterranean fare and Eastern-inspired dishes.

9 Anise
MAP E3 ■ InterContinental,
Dubai Festival City ■ 04 701 1131
■ Open 6:30pm–11:30pm ■ DD

Enjoy international fare after some shopping at Dubai Festival City Mall (see p46).

10 Nomad
MAP E2 ■ Jumeirah Creekside
Hotel, Garhoud ■ 04 230 8572
■ Open 6:30am–midnight daily
■ DD

This one-of-a-kind eatery offers a unique experience with its combination of international cuisine and a vibrant, atmospheric décor.

See map on p58

🔟 **Bur Dubai**

This bustling part of the city is packed with hotels, office blocks and residential developments, yet over a century ago it was a sandy area filled with *barasti* (palm frond houses) and windtower houses around the creek. To get a sense of old Bur Dubai visit the historical Al Fahidi neighbourhood (formerly Al Bastakiya), where the charming courtyard houses have been restored beside the creek. This atmospheric district is a quiet oasis amidst the city's hustle and bustle. Here too is the Al Fahidi Fort, now the Dubai Museum. The Shindagha heritage area, right at the creek mouth, is where Dubai's role as an enterprising and cosmopolitan trading city really began. The souks of Bur Dubai are evidence of this.

Panel detail, Architecture Museum

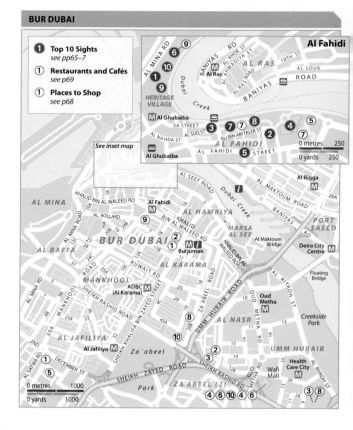

BUR DUBAI

① **Top 10 Sights** see pp65–7

① **Restaurants and Cafés** see p69

① **Places to Shop** see p68

1 Crossroads of Civilization Museum

MAP J1 ▪ Al Khaleej Road ▪ 04 393 4440 ▪ Open 10am–4pm Sat–Thu ▪ Adm ▪ www.themuseum.ae

Travel through the ages at this intimate museum. Interesting displays showcase a world-class array of largely Middle Eastern artifacts, which range from ancient Mesopotamia through to the Ottoman era. Highlights include Egyptian mummy masks, priceless Sumerian sculptures and a beautiful section of *kiswa* (cloth used to drape the Kaaba in the Grand Mosque at Mecca), which was donated by legendary Ottoman ruler Suleiman the Magnificent in 1543.

2 Dubai Museum and Al Fahidi Fort

Once Dubai's main defence outpost, the imposing sand-coloured Al Fahidi Fort was built in 1788 and has also served as a jail and the ruler's residence. Renovated in 1970, it is now the city museum and worth a look for an informative overview of the Emirates' history. It makes an entertaining visit for all ages: you can walk through a souk from the 1950s, visit an oasis with a *falaj* (irrigation channel), learn about the desert at night and visit a traditional *barasti* (see pp14–15).

3 Iranian Mosque

MAP J1

Tucked away in a backstreet off the Textile Souk (see p66), Bur Dubai's superb Iranian Mosque (no entrance to non-Muslims) is tricky to find

Door at the Iranian Mosque

but well worth the effort. Following the traditional Persian style, every inch of the building's façade and dome is covered in rich *girih*-style tilework glazed with swathes of deep-blue patterns and embellished with delicate arabesques and swirling floral motifs picked out in yellow and green.

4 Ruler's Court (Diwan)

MAP K2 ▪ Adjacent to Al Fahidi, Creekside

A cream building with imposing wind-towers sits beside the Creek next to the Grand Mosque. The striking gold-topped wrought-iron gates give a clue to its importance: it is the seat of power and the Ruler's Court or *Diwan*, (Persian for couch). Dubai's ruler Sheikh Mohammed's offices are here.

Ruler's Court (Diwan) beside the Creek

5 Al Fahidi

This is one of the oldest and most atmospheric heritage areas in Dubai. Here you can wander the alleyways between original, restored courtyard houses. Many are crowned with tall windtowers, which were the earliest forms of air conditioning. Late afternoon is the best time to spend a couple of hours here, when the light throws the architecture into golden relief. The area has become a cultural hub for the city with many buildings converted to art galleries and courtyard cafés (see pp18–19).

Beautiful carpets at the Textile Souk

6 Heritage Village and Diving Village

MAP K1 ▪ Al Shindagha ▪ 04 393 7151 ▪ Open 8:30am–10pm

A microcosm of Dubai's cultural and historic past, located near the mouth of the creek in the old Shindagha conservation area, this traditional complex is a living museum staffed by potters and weavers practising crafts as they have for centuries. There's a tented Bedouin village, armoury displays, handicraft shops, camel rides and an exhibition of Emirati cooking techniques. The Diving Village focuses on Dubai's sea-faring and pearl-diving history, with displays of *dhows* and black and white photographs.

Artifact from the Heritage Village

7 Textile Souk

At the heart of Bur Dubai, the Textile Souk begins at the water's edge by the Dubai Old Souk Abra Station. Since the souk's renovation, it is now housed under an imposing arcaded wooden roof, keeping it cool even during the most consuming heat. It's a mix of old and new – here you'll find moneychangers, textiles, bargain clothes, glittery Arabian slippers and curios. The souk (sometimes referred to as the "Old Souk") is great fun to explore – look out for the tailors working on old-fashioned sewing machines. Lanes off the main drag are dotted with examples of local traditional architecture, including long wooden balconies, latticed windows and the occasional windtower (see p27).

8 Hindi Lane

MAP K1

Buried away at the back of the Textile Souk, this truly delightful "Hindi Lane" (as it is known locally) is one of Dubai's best-hidden secrets. Walking into this narrow little lane is like stepping into India itself, with its colourful shops selling religious posters, garlands of flowers and bindis, and other subcontinental paraphernalia. There is even a tiny Sikh temple tucked away above the shops.

MAKTOUM FAMILY'S SETTLEMENT ON DUBAI CREEK

The Maktoum family's reign as rulers of Dubai began in 1833, when Sheikh Maktoum bin Buti and around 800 tribesmen broke away from the Bani Yas tribe of Abu Dhabi. They settled in Shindagha, an ideal location for trade and for the development of Dubai's pearling and fishing industries.

⑨ Traditional Architecture Museum

MAP J1 ■ Al Shindagha waterfront ■ Open 8am–2pm Sun–Thu ■ 04 392 0093 ■ www.dubaiculture.gov.ae

Housed in the beautiful old mansion of Sheikh Juma, this truly excellent museum has absorbing displays on the architecture of Dubai and the UAE. Displays cover the different building materials used – stone, mud, coral stone and gypsum – and traditional construction techniques. There are also exhibits of old tools and life-size mannequins of builders at work.

⑩ Sheikh Saeed Al-Maktoum House

MAP J1 ■ Al Shindagha ■ 04 393 7139 ■ Open 8am–8:30pm Sat–Thu, 3–9:30pm Fri ■ Adm

Built in 1896 from coral stone covered in lime and sand plaster, this was the home of Dubai's former ruler until his death in 1958. Opened as a museum in 1986, it contains photographs, coins, stamps and documents. The building itself has four windtowers and verandas. Photographs from the 1950s to the 1980s show seaplanes landing in the creek and reveal the extraordinary pace of development. Copies of early oil prospecting agreements with international companies make fascinating reading on the Trucial Coast "oil rush".

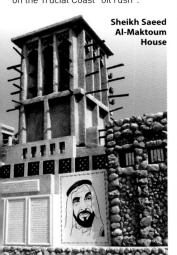

Sheikh Saeed Al-Maktoum House

A DAY'S EXPLORATION OF OLD DUBAI

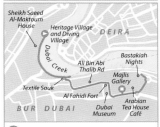

▶ **MORNING**

Start your tour at the **Heritage Village and Diving Village** at 10am, where you can learn about Emirati crafts and the history of Dubai's pearling industry. Take a break to sample fresh lemon and mint juice at any of the nearby waterside restaurants.

Afterwards, head in the opposite direction to explore the rest of the Shindagha heritage area *(see pp16–17)*, including a visit to the museum within **Sheikh Saeed Al-Maktoum House**. Following the curve of the creek, you will arrive at the wooden-arcaded **Textile Souk**. Enjoy a browse of the textile and curio stalls here. Also peep down the alleyways for views of restored windtowers and small fabric and tailor shops. At the end of the first covered section of the souk, head left to the creek for a great view across to **Deira Spice Souk** *(see p26)*. Wend your way through to Ali Bin Abi Thalib Rd and to your right is the unmistakable **Dubai Museum** and **Al Fahidi Fort** *(see p65)*, where you can easily spend an interesting, informative hour.

AFTERNOON

Head along Al-Fahidi St to the Al Fahidi area where you can enjoy a leisurely courtyard lunch inside the restored building of the **Arabian Tea House Café** *(see pp18–19)*. Afterwards, spend some time exploring Al Fahidi's alleys and buildings; don't miss authentic cuisine at **Bastakiah Nights** *(see p18–19)* and the bijou **Majlis Gallery** *(see p38)*.

See map on p64

Places to Shop

Burjuman Mall, spread out over several stylish levels

(1) Burjuman Mall
MAP J3 ▪ Trade Centre Rd ▪ 04 352 0222 ▪ Open 10am–midnight
This chic shopping mall has high-end stores selling exclusive labels and glam accessories.

(2) Jashanmal "Around the World"
MAP J3 ▪ Burjuman Mall ▪ 04 325 4698 ▪ Open 10am–10pm Sat–Wed, 10am–11pm Thu & Fri
Offering bags, suitcases and accessories from multiple brands, this is Dubai's best store for travel requirements.

(3) Lamcy Plaza
MAP H4 ▪ Adjacent to Sheikh Rashid Rd–Um Hurair Rd interchange ▪ 04 335 9999 ▪ Open 10am–11pm Sat–Wed, 10am–midnight Thu & Fri
A long-established mall where you'll find everyday practical items at very affordable prices.

(4) Wafi Gourmet
MAP H5 ▪ Wafi City ▪ 04 324 4433 ▪ Open 10am–10pm Sat–Wed, 10am–midnight Thu & Fri
Stocked with Arabian cheeses and sweets, barrels of olives and dates, plus boxes of Lebanese delights, this is Dubai's favourite delicatessen.

(5) Satwa
MAP E2
This suburb is known for its fabrics, tailors and Indian sweet shops – it is where the local people go to shop.

(6) Wafi City
MAP E2 ▪ Oud Metha Rd ▪ 04 324 4555 ▪ Open 10am–10pm Sat–Wed, 10am–midnight Thu–Fri
This kitsch, Egyptian-themed, pyramid-shaped building is the very best place to head if you love fashion.

(7) Textile Souk
Wander through this old renovated souk with small shops and stalls selling a medley of goods, from textiles and shoes to bargain clothing and curios (see p66).

(8) Karama Souk
Hunt for cheap Arabian souvenirs, handicrafts and fake designer goods at this shopping complex. For an authentic sense of local life, wander around the gritty neighbourhood afterwards (see p27).

(9) Computer Plaza
MAP F7 ▪ Al-Ain Centre ▪ 04 358 1020 ▪ Open 10am–10pm
This shopping centre, with over 60 specialized retail outlets, is the perfect place to pick up a discounted laptop or digital camera. A range of software is also available.

(10) Ajmal
MAP J3 ▪ Burjuman Mall ▪ 04 351 5505 ▪ Open 10am–10pm Sat–Wed, 10am–11pm Thu & Fri
Specializing in Arabic perfumes, which are stronger and spicier than Western fragrances, this store will mix you a signature scent.

Restaurants and Cafés

1 Ravi
MAP E4 ▪ Satwa Roundabout
▪ Open 5am–3am ▪ No alcohol ▪ D

With its famed butter chicken, Ravi is something of an institution. An inexpensive local favourite, this eatery serves Pakistani cuisine, and keeps the people of the city well fed. The tables are always packed.

2 Lemongrass
MAP H4 ▪ Near Lamcy Plaza
▪ 04 334 2325 ▪ Open noon–11:30pm
▪ No alcohol ▪ DD

An innovative and affordable Thai restaurant where you can savour some fresh, authentic dishes.

3 Manhattan Grill
MAP E2 ▪ Grand Hyatt ▪ 04 317 2222 ▪ Open 12:30–3pm & 7–11:30pm ▪ DDD

Dig into high-quality juicy steaks at this top-end American diner-style restaurant. Set menu and vegetarian options are available too, and there is a really superb wine list.

4 Khan Murjan
MAP E2 ▪ Souk Khan Murjan, Wafi ▪ 04 327 9795 ▪ Open 10am–12:30am ▪ DD

A lovely courtyard restaurant that locals flock to for fantastic Arabian food. Dishes range from Lebanese staples through to Egyptian, Moroccan and Iranian classics, alongside some traditional Gulf dishes.

5 Bastakiah Nights
With its rooftop offering unrivalled views of old Dubai, this real gem of a restaurant is a must-visit for authentic Arabic and Emirati cuisine (see p19).

6 Marcos
MAP E2 ▪ Wafi City ▪ 04 324 4100 ▪ Open noon–3pm & 7pm–midnight ▪ DD

This stylish restaurant serves scrumptious Italian dishes in a chic setting.

PRICE CATEGORIES

For a three-course meal for one with half a bottle of wine (or equivalent meal), taxes and extra charges.

D Under AED 100 DD AED 100–400
DDD Over AED 400

7 Arabian Tea House Café
MAP K2 ▪ 04 353 5071 ▪ Open 8am–10pm

For a sense of Arabia, enjoy lunch at this alcohol-free, bougainvillea-clad historic courtyard (see p19).

8 Peppercrab
MAP E2 ▪ Grand Hyatt Dubai ▪ 04 317 2222 ▪ Open 7–11:30pm (till 1am Thu & Fri) ▪ DDD

Devour a tasty, peppery crab at this Singaporean seafood restaurant (aprons and pliers are provided).

9 Kan Zaman
MAP K1 ▪ Heritage Village ▪ 04 324 3000 ▪ Open 9am–11pm ▪ No alcohol ▪ D

Great Arabic fare in a creekside setting. Watch the water taxis while you enjoy mezze and fresh juices.

10 Asha's
MAP E2 ▪ Pyramids Wafi City ▪ 04 324 4100 ▪ Open noon–3pm & 7:30pm–midnight ▪ DDD

Owned by Bollywood singing sensation Asha Bhosle, this chic restaurant has a loyal local following for its Indian classics and daring creations.

Asha's eye-catching interior

See map on p64

TOP 10 Sheikh Zayed Road and Downtown Dubai

Dubai's key artery, Sheikh Zayed Road, is a defining symbol of the city's meteoric development, flanked with a giddying array of soaring skyscrapers of every imaginable shape and size. Even Sheikh Zayed Road's futuristic skyline, however, is eclipsed by the record-breaking Downtown Dubai development just to the south. Here you'll find some of the city's most ambitious modern mega-developments, including the world's largest mall, its biggest fountain, and the Burj Khalifa, the tallest building on the planet.

The gleaming Emirates Tower

1 Emirates Towers
MAP D6 ■ Sheikh Zayed Rd
■ 04 319 8999

Two triangular twin towers, clad in aluminium and silver glass, soar into the Sheikh Zayed Road's skyline: the Jumeirah Emirates Towers. The taller is an office block, where Dubai ruler Sheikh Mohammed bin Rashid Al Maktoum has his office, and the other a 400-bedroom luxury hotel joined by a central podium containing a shopping boulevard. The hotel and boulevard have a great choice of restaurants and bars. Shopping options include international fashion from top designers, jewellery and antiques.

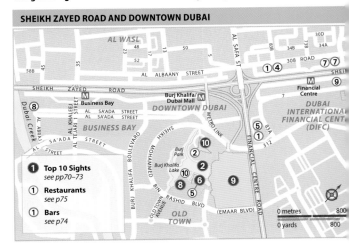

SHEIKH ZAYED ROAD AND DOWNTOWN DUBAI

① **Top 10 Sights**
see pp70–73

① **Restaurants**
see p75

① **Bars**
see p74

0 metres 800
0 yards 800

Dubai Fountain puts on a display

2 Dubai Fountain

MAP C6 ■ **Displays daily every 30 min at 6–11pm, plus 1pm & 1:30pm (except Fri)**

Filling the space between the Burj Khalifa, Dubai Mall and Souk al Bahar is the spectacular Dubai Fountain, the world's largest, featuring an extraordinary array of jets illuminated with 6,000 lights and capable of firing plumes of water 150 m (492 ft) into the air. Set in the middle of a lake, the fountain puts on an amazing show after dusk when colourful sprays of water erupt dancing in time to an accompanying musical soundtrack.

3 Dubai World Trade Centre

MAP E5 ■ Sheikh Zayed Rd ■ 04 332 1000 ■ www.dwtc.com

Hard to believe today when you see it dwarfed by the skyscrapers of Sheikh Zayed Rd, but back in 1979 the DWTC was the tallest building in the city, opened with great pomp by Sheikh Rashid and Queen Elizabeth II of England. It has played an important role in the city's development, a fact reflected by the continued use of its image on the AED 100 note. Today, it also comprises 14 huge exhibition halls. The Dubai International Convention Centre next door can accommodate more than 10,000.

4 DIFC and the Gate

MAP D6 ■ Sheikh Zayed Rd ■ 04 362 2222

Behind Emirates Towers is the Gate, the striking 15-storey architectural signature of the Dubai International Financial Centre (DIFC). This "city within a city" is now a global financial hub with its own civil and commercial laws. The Gate is shaped like a bridge – DIFC is designed to bridge the gap between the financial centres of London and New York in the West and Hong Kong and Tokyo in the East. The attached Gate Village is stuffed with upmarket galleries.

DIFC and the Gate

Flamingos at Ras Al Khor Sanctuary

5 Ras Al Khor Wildlife Sanctuary

MAP E2 ■ Ras Al Khor ■ 04 606 6822 ■ Open 9am–4pm Sat–Thu ■ Free entry to the hides; groups of more than 10 require permits

Pink flamingos, waders and other birds can be viewed on a marshy reserve at the inner end of Dubai Creek. This urban reserve has two hides: Flamingo and Mangrove. Both are fitted out with telescopes, binoculars and picture panels.

6 Souk Al Bahar

MAP C6 ■ Sheikh Zayed Rd ■ Open 10am–10pm Sat–Thu, 2–10pm Fri ■ www.soukalbahar.ae

Next to the futuristic Burj Khalifa is a slice of old, albeit newly built, Arabia. Souk Al Bahar is an Arabesque shopping mall with over 100 retail outlets including independent boutiques, souvenir shops and antique stores.

Along the souk's pleasant waterfront promenade there is also a host of eateries, from upscale restaurants to cafés and lounge bars. This is the perfect spot for a stroll before you attempt the shopping madness of the Dubai Mall, which is just a few minutes' walk away.

7 Meydan Stable Tour

MAP D2 ■ Meydan Racecourse ■ 04 381 3405 ■ Open Sep–Apr ■ www.stabletours.meydan.ae

The tour of this world-class facility includes the chance to observe thoroughbred training in action. The morning tour starts at 7am with a trackside breakfast, after which you are given a behind-the-scenes look at the saddling paddock, jockeys' lounge, parade ring and the glamorous VIP suites that play host to royals and celebrities.

8 The Palace

MAP C6 ■ Downtown Burj Khalifa ■ 04 428 7888 ■ www.the address.com

Tucked away behind Souk al Bahar is the opulent Palace hotel. The hotel's exquisite Arabian-style façade and palm-lined ornamental pool are sights in their own right, made all the more memorable by the hotel's incongruous juxtaposition with the futuristic Burj Khalifa (see pp12–13) rising directly behind. The hotel's Thiptara restaurant (see p75) offers fine Thai dining and peerless views of the Dubai Fountain.

Exterior of the Palace

9 **The Dubai Mall**
MAP C6 ■ Next to the Burj Khalifa ■ Open 10am–10pm Sun–Wed, 10am–midnight Thu–Sat ■ www.thedubaimall.com

The ultimate shrine to consumerism, this mall has a vast array of shops and other attractions, including the Dubai Aquarium, an ice rink and a skeleton of a 150-million-year-old diplodocus dinosaur. Highlights include the Arabian-themed souk section and the ultra-chic Fashion Avenue. The selection of places to eat include some nice alfresco places overlooking the Dubai Fountain.

The Dubai Mall, a retail heaven

10 **Burj Khalifa**
Named after the UAE president Sheikh Khalifa bin Zayed Al Nahyan, the Burj Khalifa is far and away the tallest man-made structure on the planet. Most of the tower is residential but a pair of observation decks are open to visitors and the base of the building houses the world's first Armani Hotel (see pp12–13).

GODOLPHIN
The famous Godolphin racing stable was established by the equestrian-loving Maktoum Royal Family of Dubai in 1994 and has won Group One races in 11 countries. It bred the great Dubai Millennium, who won the Dubai World Cup 2000 by over six lengths and sired 59 offspring (see www.godolphin.com).

A STROLL AMONGST THE SKYSCRAPERS

▶ MORNING

Begin the morning with a stroll down **Sheikh Zayed Road** (see pp12–13), starting at the **Emirates Towers** (see p70) and admiring the area's many super-tall sky-scrapers. **Shakespeare & Co** (see p75), about halfway down the strip, is a great place to get some breakfast or a coffee. Head on to the **Dubai Mall** and spend time exploring the shops here. If shopping doesn't appeal, there are plenty of other attractions at the mall, including the Dubai Aquarium or the chance to go for a cooling spin at the ice rink. Lunch can be found in one of the mall's myriad cafés.

AFTERNOON

After lunch head to the pretty, Arabian-themed **Souk Al Bahar**, where more shops await. Then pop into **the Palace** hotel for tea before making a late afternoon visit to the observation deck of the **Burj Khalifa** for Dubai's most amazing views (be sure to reserve tickets in advance).

As dusk begins to fall, go out onto the promenade surrounding **Burj Khalifa Lake** (see p12) and watch the show-stopping **Dubai Fountain** spring into life. Next, head to **the Address Boulevard** (04 423 8888) and enjoy a snack at the sophisticated lobby lounge that features a selection of gourmet sandwiches, scones and handpicked signature blends. Alternatively, head to the oriental-style **Karma Kafé** (see p75) in Souk Al Bahar or to one of the many waterside restaurants to end your Downtown Dubai day with dinner.

Bars

1 Double Decker
MAP C6 ■ Roda Al Murooj Hotel, Financial Centre Rd ■ 04 321 1111 ■ Open 12pm–3am

A lively pub with decor themed after the famous London red Routemaster buses. The programme of music and other events keeps things busy.

2 Alta Badia Bar
MAP D6 ■ Emirates Towers Hotel ■ 04 319 8771 ■ Open 6pm–3am ■ www.jumeirah.com

This sophisticated bar has unbeatable views and a good range of cocktails.

3 Cin Cin's
MAP E5 ■ Fairmont Hotel ■ 04 311 8316 ■ Open 7pm–2am ■ www.fairmont.com

This chic champagne bar has a great snack menu with freshly-shucked oysters and Wagyu beefburgers.

4 The Balcony Bar
MAP C5 ■ Shangri-La Hotel ■ 04 405 2703 ■ Open 9am–3am

An ideal place to unwind, this swanky restaurant overlooks the hotel's chic lobby. Enjoy an array of drinks while soaking up the ambience.

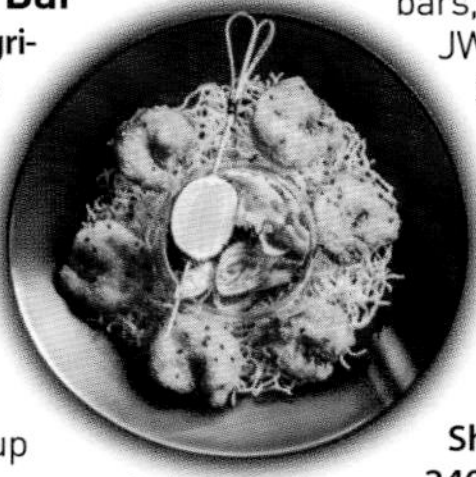

A dish on the menu at Vault

5 Asia Asia
MAP B2 ■ Pier 7, Dubai Marina ■ 04 276 5900 ■ Open 4pm–1am Sat–Wed, 4pm–2am Thu & Fri ■ www.asia-asia.com

An urbane dining destination, this restaurant serves pan-Asian cuisine inspired by exotic places such as Thailand, Shanghai, and Kyoto.

6 Blue Bar
MAP E5 ■ Novotel Hotel, behind World Trade Centre ■ 04 332 0000 ■ Open 12pm–2am

A low-key relaxed bar where you can chill to the tunes of the resident band.

Colonial-style interior at Long's Bar

7 Long's Bar
MAP D5 ■ Towers Rotana Hotel ■ 04 312 2202 ■ Open 12pm–1am ■ www.rotana.com

This colonial-style bar, with its small dance floor, claims to have the longest bar in the whole of the UAE.

8 Vault
MAP B6 ■ Business Bay ■ 04 414 3000 ■ Open 5pm–3am ■ www.jwmarriottmarquisdubailife.com

Vault is one of the world's highest bars, on the 72nd floor of the JW Marriott Marquis hotel. Svelte decor and the upmarket ambience are complemented by sweeping views through 360° windows.

9 Fibber McGees
MAP D5 ■ Off Sheikh Zayed Rd ■ 04 332 2400 ■ Open 8am–2am ■ www.fibbersdubai.com.

Dubai's best traditional pub is tricky to find (check directions on the website) but worth the effort. The homely interior transports you straight to Ireland, as do the draught Kilkenny and Guinness. There's good food, too, plus regular live music.

10 Zinc
MAP E5 ■ Crowne Plaza Hotel ■ 04 331 1111 ■ Open 10pm–3am ■ www.crowneplaza.com

Always packed, this popular bar and club has an ever-changing line-up of live music and local DJs playing a variety of music genres.

Restaurants

1 Hoi An
MAP C5 ■ Shangri-La Hotel, Sheikh Zayed Rd ■ 04 343 8888 ■ Open 7pm–midnight ■ DDD
Vietnamese fare served in elegant surroundings with a range of dishes and excellent service *(see p47)*.

2 At.mosphere
MAP C6 ■ 122nd Floor, Burj Khalifa ■ 04 888 3828 ■ Open 12:30–3pm, 6:30–11:30pm daily (until 2am in the lounge bar) ■ DDD
The world's highest restaurant, this place offers top-notch European-style fine dining in incredible surroundings on the 122nd floor of the Burj Khalifa.

3 Alta Badia
MAP D6 ■ Emirates Towers ■ 04 319 8771 ■ Open noon–3pm & 6–midnight ■ DDD
This elegant restaurant on the 51st floor serves authentic Italian cuisine. Try to get a table by the window.

4 Exchange Grill
MAP E5 ■ Fairmont Hotel ■ 04 332 5555 ■ Open 7pm–midnight ■ DDD
Visit the best steakhouse in town, which serves delicious melt-in-the mouth Kobo steak.

5 Karma Kafé
MAP C6 ■ Souk Al Bahar, Downtown Burj Khalifa ■ 04 423 0909 ■ Open 3pm–1am ■ DD
Enjoy classic Asian fusion food in the plush interior or on the lovely terrace

PRICE CATEGORIES
For a three-course meal for one with half a bottle of wine (or equivalent meal), taxes and extra charges.
....
D Under AED 100 **DD** AED 100–400
DDD Over AED 400

overlooking the magnificent Burj Khalifa and the Dubai Fountain.

6 Al Nafoorah
MAP E6 ■ Emirates Towers Boulevard ■ 04 319 8760 ■ Open noon–3:30pm & 6–11:30pm ■ DD
This smart basement restaurant is a contender for Dubai's best Arabian restaurant. Food includes immaculate mezze, succulent grills and fish, and there's a sheesha tent.

7 Teatro
MAP D5 ■ Towers Rotana Hotel ■ 04 343 8000 ■ Open 6pm–2am ■ DD
The great cross-Continental dishes here have made this restaurant a firm favourite for many years.

8 Noodle House
MAP D6 ■ Emirates Towers Boulevard ■ 04 319 8757 ■ Open noon–midnight ■ DD
Visit this place for a quick, affordable and very tasty bowl of spicy noodles.

9 Shakespeare & Co
MAP D6 ■ Al Saqr Business Tower, 37th St, off Sheikh Zayed Rd ■ 04 331 1757 ■ Open 7am–midnight ■ DD
Characterized by quirky 19th-century parlour-style decor, this restaurant serves Western and Arabian cuisine.

10 Thiptara
MAP C6 ■ The Palace Hotel, Old Town ■ 04 428 7961 ■ Open 6–11:30pm ■ DDD
Set in a beautiful wooden pavilion on the lakeside, this fine-dining restaurant specializes in Thai seafood. Reservations are recommended.

Oriental decor in the Karma Kafé

See map on pp70–71

🔟 Jumeirah

Stretching down the coast southwest from the port area, Jumeirah is one of the most glamorous and sought-after of all the city suburbs. It's no surprise that residential property here is pricey – it's the ultimate location for a place in the sun and the quiet leafy streets are filled with bougainvillea-clad luxury villas. At the southern end of the district the endless low-rise suburbs are punctuated by three of the city's most famous landmarks: the iconic "seven-star" Burj Al Arab Jumeirah, the enormous wave-shaped Jumeirah Beach Hotel and the vast mock-Arabian Madinat Jumeirah complex (home to the beautiful Souk Madinat Jumeirah). Staying here is an expensive pleasure, but the area's beaches, bars and restaurants are amongst the finest in the city, while the Wild Wadi Water Park offers watery thrills and spills for those energetic enough to leave the beach.

The Burj Al Arab Jumeirah

1 Burj Al Arab Jumeirah

Visible from almost anywhere in Jumeirah, the Burj Al Arab Jumeirah, an iconic luxury hotel, is a symbol for the city itself and is distinguished by its unusual shape mirroring the billowing sail of a *dhow*. Reservations are needed to visit the interior of this opulent hotel *(see pp24–5)*. For a great close-up view of the exterior, drop into the Jumeirah Beach Hotel and take the super-fast glass elevator to the top floor *(see p113)*.

JUMEIRAH

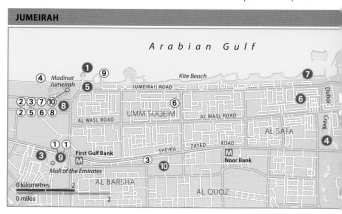

Jumeirah Mosque, a fine example of modern Islamic architecture

2 Jumeirah Mosque

Rising proudly above Jumeirah Road, the imposing Fatimid-style Jumeirah Mosque is one of the city's most impressive and attractive mosques *(see pp20–21)*.

3 Ski Dubai Snow Park

MAP C2 ■ Mall of the Emirates
■ 04 409 4000 ■ Open 10am–11pm Sun–Wed, 10am–midnight Thu–Sat
■ Adm ■ www.skidxb.com

You can't miss Ski Dubai from the Sheikh Zayed Road, jutting out like a giant space-age tube. Filled with over 6,000 tonnes of snow, it offers five slopes, linked by chairlifts and tow lifts, to cater to all ski levels, including the longest black indoor run in the world. There's also a snow park for little ones, plus the chance to meet the resident Gentoo penguins *(see p42)*.

4 Safa Park

MAP A5

A ride on the giant Ferris wheel here offers the best views of this huge landscaped green park stretching from Al Wasl Road to Sheikh Zayed Road (although construction work on the Dubai Canal has reduced the size). It is hugely popular with local residents, many of whom make the most of its specially-sprung perimeter jogging track. It's great for kids to run free and there's lots of entertainment, including a mini-train, a merry-go-round and a lake with rowing boats.

Verdant and leafy Safa Park

Attractions at Wild Wadi Water Park

5 Wild Wadi Water Park

MAP C2 ■ Jumeirah Rd ■ 04 348 4444 ■ Mar–May & Sep–Oct: 10am–7pm; Jun–Aug: 10am–8pm; Nov–Feb: 10am–6pm ■ Adm ■ www.wildwadi.com ■ Cashless payment system using electronic waterproof wristband

This world-class water park offers a great day out to suit all ages and bravery levels with 30 water-fuelled rides and attractions. Thrill-seekers will not be disappointed by its most challenging ride, the Jumeirah Sceirah – the tallest and fastest free-fall water slide outside the US. Well-staffed by lifeguards and with plenty of food outlets, it makes a fun day out.

6 Majlis Ghorfat um al Sheef

MAP D2 ■ 17 St ■ 04 226 0286 ■ 8:30am–10:30pm Sun–Thu, 3–10pm Fri & Sat ■ Adm

Hidden amongst the suburban sprawl, the Majlis Ghorfat um al Sheef is the only historic building to survive outside the old city centre. Built in 1955, this quaint two-storey structure served as a summer retreat for visionary former ruler Sheikh Rashid, with sleeping quarters below and a *majlis* (meeting room) above. The garden has date palm trees watered using traditional *falaj* irrigation channels.

7 Jumeirah Beach Park

MAP A4

This lovely green park (closed for renovation until late 2017), backs onto a beautiful white-sand beach. You can access the beach from the park along wooden walkways and there is plenty of shade on the sand under the palm trees. It's equipped with lifeguards, and has good facilities and some small cafés.

Shoreline at Jumeirah Beach Park

8 Madinat Jumeirah
MAP C2 ■ Al Sufouh Rd

This vast leisure and entertainment complex is a major focus of the Jumeirah area. It has three hotels linked by waterways navigated by silent battery-powered *abras*. There are more than 45 restaurants, bars and cafés, many with waterside views, with the seafood restaurant Pierchic *(see p81)* on a pier that stretches into the Arabian Gulf. Here also is the Souk Madinat Jumeirah *(see p80)*, a reconstruction of a traditional Arabian bazaar.

Abras at Madinat Jumeirah

9 Mall of the Emirates
MAP C2 ■ Interchange 4 ■ 04 409 9000 ■ www.mallofthe emirates.com

Dubai's swankiest retail complex has more than 500 shops, selling every product you can possibly dream of. There's also a Harvey Nichols and Debenhams. Other attractions include a multi-screen cinema and kids' play area Magic Planet *(see p42)*, plus dozens of cafés and restaurants.

10 Al Quoz Galleries
MAP C2 ■ www.alserkal avenue.ae

The gritty industrial area of Al Quoz is one of Dubai's more unlikely attractions thanks to the cutting-edge art galleries that have moved into the area. Many local galleries are relocating into the Alserkal Avenue arts centre on Street 8, including leading names like Gallery Isabelle van den Eynde and Green Art Gallery *(see pp38–9)*.

A DAY BY THE SEA

▶ MORNING

Start your day with breakfast on the outdoor terrace of **Lime Tree Café** *(see p81)*. Enjoy the gentle morning sun as you sip on some coffee or a juice. Then take an insightful morning tour of the **Jumeirah Mosque** *(see pp20–21)* for the chance to look inside one of Dubai's finest Islamic buildings. Drive or hire a taxi to **Jumeirah Beach Park**, where you can take a safe swim or laze about on a sunbed under the palm trees.

AFTERNOON

Leave at lunchtime and head to **Madinat Jumeirah**, where you can enjoy a leisurely late lunch at a huge choice of restaurants, many overlooking the waterways. Afterwards spend an hour or two window-shopping for souvenirs or browsing the lovely Arabian-style **Souk Madinat Jumeirah** *(see p80)* here.

As evening approaches, head to one of Dubai's most beautiful bars, the **Bahri Bar** *(see p81)* housed in the luxurious Mina A'Salam hotel *(see p113)*. From this beautiful alfresco spot, you can sip a cocktail whilst enjoying superb views of the **Burj Al Arab Jumeirah** and watching the sun set over the Gulf. There are numerous places to eat dinner nearby, but for pure romance head to the delectable **Pai Thai** *(see p81)* in the nearby Dar al Masyaf hotel. With fine Thai cuisine in a magical setting which overlooks the meandering water-ways of the Medinat and the Burj, a meal here is hard to beat. It is recommended to book in advance.

See map on pp76–7

Places to Shop

1 Mall of the Emirates
Prepare to shop until you drop at one of the biggest shopping centres in the region (see p79).

2 Camel Company
MAP C2 ■ Souk Madinat Jumeirah ■ 04 368 6048 ■ Open 10am–11pm ■ www.camelcompany.ae
Dubai's cutest selection of cuddly toy camels and other dromedary-themed souvenirs – perfect for kids.

3 Times Square Center
MAP C2 ■ Sheikh Zayed Rd ■ 04 341 8020 ■ Open 10am–10pm ■ www.timessquarecenter.ae
This smallish mall features an impressive electronics store. It also has its very own ice lounge where everything, from the tables to the glasses, is made out of ice.

4 The Village Mall
MAP D4 ■ Jumeirah Rd ■ 04 344 9514 ■ Open 10am–10pm Sat–Thu, 2–10pm Fri
An intriguing mix of niche upmarket boutiques fill this pretty shopping centre, with its archways, plants and fountains. It is the perfect place to find a one-of-a-kind gift.

5 Souk Madinat Jumeirah
MAP C2 ■ Al Sufouh Rd ■ Open 10am–11pm
This magical bazaar has art, jewellery, antiques and handicrafts, interspersed with great bars and restaurants.

Souk Madinat Jumeirah

6 Pride of Kashmir
MAP C2 ■ Souk Madinat Jumeirah ■ 04 368 6110 ■ Open 10am–11pm ■ www.prideof kashmir.com
A craft and souvenir shop packed with antique and modern rugs from Iran, Kashmir and Turkey.

7 Boxpark
MAP D2 ■ Al Wasl Rd ■ Open 10am–10pm (till midnight Thu–Sat) ■ www.boxpark.ae
A funky retail space made up of minimalist cuboid buildings with the odd shipping container poking out, housing eclectic and offbeat shops.

8 Gallery One
MAP C2 ■ Souk Madinat Jumeirah ■ 04 368 6055 ■ Open 10am–11pm ■ www.g-1.com
This commercial gallery specializes in selling beautiful but relatively affordable limited-edition Arabian- and Asian-themed artworks.

9 Mercato Mall
MAP C4 ■ Jumeirah Beach Rd ■ 04 344 4161 ■ Open 10am–10pm ■ www.mercatoshoppingmall.com
An Italian-themed mall with 90 shops, restaurants and cafés. With a fun soft play area, it is great for kids.

10 Jumeirah Plaza
MAP D4 ■ Jumeirah Rd ■ 04 349 0766 ■ Open 10am–10pm Sat–Thu, 1:30–10pm Fri
This small mall, popular with local residents, has a pleasant coffee shop with an outdoor terrace.

Restaurants and Bars

PRICE CATEGORIES

For a three-course meal for one with half a bottle of wine (or equivalent meal), taxes and extra charges.

D Under AED 100 DD AED 100–400
DDD Over AED 400

1 Almaz by Momo
MAP C2 ▪ Mall of the Emirates ▪ 04 409 8877 ▪ Open 10am–1am ▪ No alcohol ▪ DD
Set up by famous restauranteur Mourad Mazouz, this is the hippest Moroccan restaurant in town.

2 Zheng He's
MAP C1 ▪ Mina A' Salem, Midinat Jumeirah ▪ 04 366 6730 ▪ Open noon–11:30am ▪ DDD
Dine on fresh seafood and Chinese cuisine by the harbourfront.

3 Trattoria Toscana
MAP C2 ▪ Madinat Jumeirah ▪ 04 366 6730 ▪ Open noon–midnight ▪ DD
Delicious Italian fare is served in a mock Venetian waterway setting.

4 Pierchic
MAP C1 ▪ Al Qasr, Madinat Jumeirah ▪ 04 366 6730 ▪ Open 12:30–3pm Sat–Fri & 6:15–midnight Sat–Sun ▪ DDD
Book a terrace table at this seafood restaurant on a wooden pier.

5 Lime Tree Café
MAP D4 ▪ Jumeirah Rd ▪ 04 348 8498 ▪ Open 7:30am–6:30pm ▪ No alcohol ▪ D
This homely café with a shady outdoor terrace serves healthy homemade lunches, soups, juices, tea and coffee.

6 Maria Bonita's Taco Shop
MAP C2 ▪ Umm Al Sheif St ▪ 04 395 5576 ▪ Open noon–midnight ▪ No alcohol ▪ D
Be transported to Mexico for good-value tacos, tortillas and salsas.

7 Bahri Bar
MAP C2 ▪ Mina A' Salam, Madinat Jumeirah ▪ 04 366 8888 ▪ Open 4pm–1am
With a large terrace and views of the Burj Al Arab Jumeirah light shows, this is an ideal spot for a sundowner.

Elegant surroundings at Bahri Bar

8 Sho Cho's
MAP E4 ▪ Dubai Marine Beach Resort & Spa ▪ 04 346 1111 ▪ Open 6pm–3am
This super-chic Japanese bar offers a gorgeous terrace overlooking the Gulf. The interior walls are filled with fish tanks.

9 360°
MAP C1 ▪ Jumeirah Beach Hotel ▪ 04 406 8741 ▪ Open 5pm–2am Sat–Thu, 4pm–3am Fri
Located in a glass building perched out at sea at the end of a breakwater, this is a great place for a sunset drink.

10 Pai Thai
MAP C2 ▪ Dar al Masyaf, Madinat Jumeirah ▪ 04 432 3232 ▪ Open 6:30–11:30pm ▪ DDD
Romance is in the air at this magical restaurant set above the Madinat Jumeirah waterways. The chic decor and memorable views from the candlelit terrace are spectacular, as is the Thai cuisine (see p47).

See map on pp76–7 ➤

TOP 10 Dubai Marina and Palm Jumeirah

Far south of the city you'll find the most evidence of modern Dubai's growth. Little over a decade ago most of this area was nothing but sand and sea. Now, it's a whole new city within a city. The skyscrapers of the Dubai Marina district run unbroken for several kilometres along the coast, enclosing a futuristic marina that is backed by a swathe of beach and huge resorts. Offshore lies the Palm Jumeirah, the world's largest artificial island, crowned by the Atlantis resort.

The marina

DUBAI MARINA AND PALM JUMEIRAH

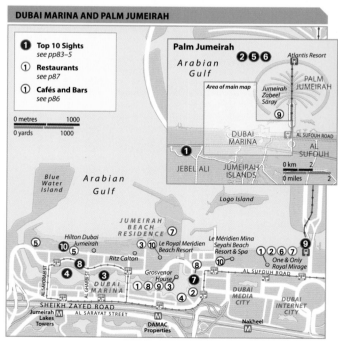

- **1** Top 10 Sights
  see pp83–5
- **1** Restaurants
  see p87
- **1** Cafés and Bars
  see p86

0 metres   1000
0 yards   1000

1 Ibn Battuta Mall
MAP A2 ■ Emirates Hills
■ 04 362 1900 ■ Open 10am–
10pm (till midnight Thu–Sat)
■ www.ibnbattutamall.com
Dubai's most bizarre mall by a
mile, the Ibn Battuta is designed
around the travels of the
legendary Moroccan traveller.
The mall is themed after six of
the countries visited by Battuta,
including a bright red Chinese
section (complete with a junk
ship), an Indian section with
a life-size replica elephant,
and a Tunisian village at
dusk. Best of all is the
Persian zone, arranged
around a spectacularly
tiled, mosque-like dome.

2 Lost Chambers
MAP B1 ■ Atlantis,
the Palm ■ 04
426 0000 ■ Open
10am–10pm
■ Adm; under 3s free
■ www.atlantisthepalm.com
Located inside Atlantis, The Palm,
the atmospheric Lost Chambers is
a vast aquarium filled with colourful
shoals of tropical fish and other
marine creatures, including sharks,
piranhas and seahorses. Assorted
fake "ruins" have been placed amid
the waters, masquerading as the
remains of the legendary ancient
Mediterranean city of Atlantis itself.

Indian elephant, Ibn Battuta Mall

3 Boat Trips at the Marina
The marina development is
definitely a place best appreciated
from the water, and there
are a range of boat trips
available to make this
possible. The cheapest
and simplest option is to
take a ride on one of the
water taxis, which shuttle
up and down the marina
itself, and there are also
after-dark dinner cruises
aboard traditional *dhows*.
Alternatively, catch a ride
on the Dubai Ferry (see
p105) that runs between
Bur Dubai and the marina
or go for a sightseeing
tour with the Yellow
Boats (see p55).

4 The Marina
MAP B2
Centrepiece of the Dubai
Marina development is the
expansive marina itself, lined
with millionaires' boats and
surrounded by skyscrapers
on all sides. It is particularly
impressive when illuminated after
dark. Created out of a man-made
sea inlet running parallel to the ocean,
the marina is the best part of 3 km
(2 miles) long. Disoriented sharks
and even whales have been known
to swim into it from time to time.

Underwater hall, Lost Chambers

Interior of Atlantis, The Palm

5 Atlantis, The Palm

Dominating the far end of the Palm Jumeirah is the vast Atlantis, The Palm resort. This is one of Dubai's most distinctive landmarks, a soaring pink colossus arranged around a vast Arabian-style archway. The lavish interior is a riot of gold columns and marble floors. Attractions include the Lost Chambers *(see p83)*, Aquaventure and Dolphin Bay, and a vast swathe of beach *(see p113)*.

6 Aquaventure and Dolphin Bay

MAP B1 ▪ Atlantis, The Palm ▪ 04 426 1030 ▪ Open 10am–sunset ▪ Adm ▪ www.atlantisthepalm.com

The Aquaventure water park offers state-of-the-art rides and attractions. The highlight is the huge Leap of Faith water slide, which lands you in a transparent tunnel in a shark-filled lagoon. The adjacent Dolphin Bay gives visitors the unforgettable opportunity to swim with the resort's resident bottlenose dolphins, offering shallow-water programmes for kids and deep-water interactions for stronger swimmers.

7 Marina Walk

MAP B2

Encircling both sides of Dubai Marina is the pedestrianized Marina Walk. An array of cafés and restaurants line the waterfront here, along with the swanky Marina Mall *(see p50)*. At the northern end of the marina, look out for the unmistakeable 73-storey Cayan Tower with its remarkable twisted shape – the entire building rotates over 90°. When this residential tower opened in 2013 it was the world's tallest high-rise building, but it has now been surpassed by the Burj Khalifa *(see pp12–13)*.

People stepping out while enjoying the views from Marina Walk

8 The Walk at JBR
MAP B2

Running along the beachfront is the Walk at JBR, a long boulevard of shops, restaurants, cafés and hotels backed by the huge towers of the Jumeirah Beach Residence, which is one of the city's most relaxed places for an outdoor stroll. Adjacent, the Beach at JBR is amongst Dubai's most attractive recent developments, with a low-rise cluster of shops and restaurants arranged around pretty piazzas and fountains.

The Palm Monorail crossing the Gulf

9 Palm Monorail
MAP B1–2 ■ Open 10am–10pm (trains every 20–30 min) ■ Adm

The only place you really get a proper view of the Palm Jumeirah is from the air. If your budget can't quite stretch to a helicopter ride, the Palm Monorail offers the best overview of the development, running on a raised track across the island and offering great views of the Palm and the skyscrapers of Dubai Marina behind.

10 Marina Beach
MAP B2

One of the marina's top draws is its superb swathe of white sand – the best free beach in the city. The size of the beach means that there's usually plenty of space to lounge on (although it does get busy, particularly at weekends) and there are various facilities including showers and changing rooms, plus loungers for hire. This is also the best place in Dubai to arrange water sports, with a wide selection of activities available, including sailing, water-skiing, kayaking and banana boats.

A DAY ON LAND AND OUT AT SEA

Atlantis Resort
Lost Chambers
Palm Jumeirah
PALM MONORAIL
Marina Beach
The Walk at JBR
Dubai Marina
One&Only Royal Mirage
TRAM
Marina Mall

▶ MORNING

Start your day by going for a pleasant stroll around **the marina** (see p83). Spend an hour or so exploring the shops in the **Marina Mall** or take a boat trip (see p83). Next, walk over to the nearby **Marina Beach**. Take some time to catch the rays or maybe try your hand at one of the water sports on offer there. Afterwards, explore the shops along **the Walk at JBR** and grab some lunch in one of the many cafés and restaurants.

AFTERNOON

After lunch, catch the Dubai tram to Palm Monorail station and ride the **Palm Monorail** across to **Atlantis, The Palm**, with bird's-eye views across the huge Palm Jumeirah along the way. Have a look around the vast Atlantis resort's lavish interior and visit the spectacular **Lost Chambers** aquarium (see p83).

EVENING

Hop back on board the monorail and head back to the mainland. From Palm Monorail station continue to the nearby **One&Only Royal Mirage** (see p113). You can spend an enjoyable evening here admiring the hotel's magical Moorish architecture and endless palm trees. Start with a drink at Moroccan-style The **Rooftop** terrace bar (see p86), followed by dinner at one of the resorts excellent restaurants. The pool-fringed **Eauzone** (see p87) is particularly romantic, but you will need to book ahead.

See map on p82 ←

Cafés and Bars

1 The Rooftop
MAP B2 ▪ Arabian Court,
One&Only Royal Mirage, Al Sufouh
▪ 04 399 9999 ▪ Open 5pm–1:30am

Visit this Moroccan-styled bar for views over the Arabian Gulf and a relaxed drink under a star-filled sky.

2 Chandelier
MAP B2 ▪ Dubai Marina
▪ 04 366 3606 ▪ Open 10am–2am
▪ No alcohol ▪ DD

This casual Lebanese restaurant is good for a light lunch or evening meal. It has a pleasant outdoor terrace, where you can also sample sheesha.

3 Bar 44
MAP B2 ▪ Grosvenor House,
Dubai Marina ▪ 04 399 8888 ▪ Open
4pm–2am Fri–Wed, 4pm–3am Thu
▪ www.bar44-dubai.com

This top-floor swanky bar with comfy sofas and a giant balcony offers 44 different types of champagne.

4 Johnny Rockets
MAP B2 ▪ Marina Walk (south),
Dubai Marina ▪ 04 368 2339 ▪ Open
10am–1am ▪ DD

Re-creating the look of a 1950s US diner, this eatery serves milkshakes and the very best burgers in town.

Diner-style interior at Johnny Rockets

5 Stereo Arcade
MAP B2 ▪ DoubleTree by
Hilton, the Walk at JBR, Dubai Marina
▪ 052 618 2424 ▪ Open 6pm–3am
▪ www.facebook.com/StereoArcade

A rustic European-style pub with an attached room full of vintage 1980s arcade video games that are free to play when you buy a drink.

6 Nasimi Beach
MAP B1 ▪ Atlantis, The Palm,
Palm Jumeirah ▪ 04 426 2626 ▪ Open
9am–1am Sun–Thu, 9am–2am Fri–Sat

With an outside terrace spilling onto the sand, what better way is there to unwind than sprawled out on a beanbag with an ice-cold drink?

7 Zero Gravity
MAP B1 ▪ Al Sufouh Rd ▪ 04
399 0009 ▪ Open 10am till late (from
8am Fri & Sat) ▪ www.0-gravity.ae ▪ D

This beachfront bar-restaurant is a lovely place to linger over a sun-downer. A selection of food is served from breakfast until late at night.

8 Masaad
MAP B2 ▪ The Walk at JBR,
Dubai Marina ▪ 04 362 9002 ▪ Open
11am–11pm ▪ www.massaadfarm
totable.com ▪ D

One of the best cheap places to eat in Dubai Marina, this tiny café dishes up excellent Arabian light meals using fresh, locally sourced ingredients.

9 Voda Bar
MAP B1 ▪ Jumeirah Zabeel
Saray, Palm Jumeirah ▪ 04 453 0444
▪ Open 6pm–3am ▪ www.jumeirah.com

Pod-like chairs and arctic-blue lighting give this funky bar the look of a futuristic ice-cavern.

10 Barasti
MAP B2 ▪ Le Meridien Mina
Seyahi Beach Resort & Marina
▪ 04 318 1313 ▪ Open 11am–3:30am

Barasti comes alive on the weekends, when revellers sprawl out across the sand. There is live music most nights.

Restaurants

1 **Buddha Bar**
Grosvenor House, Dubai Marina
■ 04 317 6833 ■ Open 7pm–midnight
■ DDD
Expect great Pan-Asian food and
cocktails at this hip restaurant with a
huge Buddha centrepiece (see p46).

Atmospheric dining at Tagine

2 **Tagine**
MAP B2 ■ One&Only Royal
Mirage, Al Sufouh ■ 04 399 9999
■ Open 7–11:30pm Tue–Sun ■ DD
Visit this candlelit restaurant for a
magical Moroccan experience. The
courtyard location adds to its charm.

3 **Maya**
MAP B2 ■ Le Royal Meridien
Beach Resort ■ 04 316 5550 ■ Open
7pm–midnight ■ DDD
Come to Maya to experience new-
wave Mexican cuisine in spacious
surroundings decorated with
Mayan art and modern sculpture.

4 **Amala**
MAP B1 ■ Jumeirah Zabeel
Saray, Palm Jumeirah ■ 04 453 0444
■ Open 6pm–1am Sun–Thu & 1–4pm
Fri–Sat ■ DD
Enjoy tasty North Indian dishes in a
lavish setting with traditional decor.

5 **BiCE**
MAP B2 ■ Hilton Dubai
Jumeirah ■ 04 399 1111 ■ Open
12:30–3:30pm & 7–11:30pm ■ DD
An Art Deco-themed Italian with
an excellent selection of seafood,
meat dishes and wine.

6 **Eauzone**
MAP B2 ■ One&Only Royal
Mirage, Al Sufouh ■ 04 399 9999
■ Open noon–3:30pm & 7–11:30pm
■ DDD
Enjoy classic Pan-Asian dishes and
contemporary fine-dining creations
at tables under tented canopies laid
out alongside a floodlit pool (see p46).

7 **Nina**
MAP B2 ■ One&Only Royal
Mirage, Al Sufouh ■ 04 399 9999
Open 7–11:30pm Mon–Sat ■ DDD
Sample traditional Indian ingredients
with a new twist at this sophisticated
restaurant in pretty surroundings.
A live DJ plays background music.

8 **Indego by Vineet**
MAP B2 ■ Grosvenor House,
Dubai Marina ■ 04 317 6000 ■ Open
7pm–midnight ■ DDD
A contemporary take on traditional
Indian cuisine overseen by chef
Vineet Bhatia, the first Indian chef to
be awarded a Michelin star (see p47).

9 **Ruya**
MAP B2 ■ Grosvenor House,
Dubai Marina ■ 04 317 6000 ■ Open
6pm–1am Sat–Wed, 6pm–2pm Thu &
Fri ■ www.ruyadubai.com ■ DD
Visit Ruya for an authentic,
contemporary Anatolian cuisine in
a lively, relaxed setting.

10 **Rhodes Twenty10**
MAP B2 ■ Le Royal Méridien
Beach Resort ■ 04 316 5550 ■ Open
7pm–midnight ■ DDD
A lively restaurant overseen by
UK chef Gary Rhodes, it features a
mix of British classics and Middle
Eastern-influenced dishes (see p47).

See map on p82

🔟 Downtown Abu Dhabi

A stunning city of shiny new skyscrapers strung out along an idyllic corniche, oil-rich Abu Dhabi is the capital of the UAE and a rising player in the world's financial, commercial and tourist stages. Many visitors enjoy the slower and more traditional pace of life compared to Dubai, although after years in the shadow of its neighbour, Abu Dhabi is now also launching into its own spectacular spate of large-scale developments, ranging from the ultra-opulent mock-Arabian Emirates Palace, one of the world's most lavish hotels, to the futuristic architecture of Al Maryah Island and the gleaming Etihad Towers. Downtown Abu Dhabi is the city's bustling commercial centre, where you'll find the biggest mega-developments, the liveliest attractions, and all the busiest shops, bars and restaurants.

The expansive Abu Dhabi Corniche

1 Abu Dhabi Corniche
MAP N1–R1

Abu Dhabi's showpiece boulevard sweeps for almost 5 km (3 miles) along the Downtown waterfront. A long line of skyscrapers rises to one side, while to the other are a series of gardens, popular in the evenings with strolling locals and joggers. Hiring a bike and riding up and down the waterfront is a great way to spend an hour or so, and there's a fine stretch of public beach.

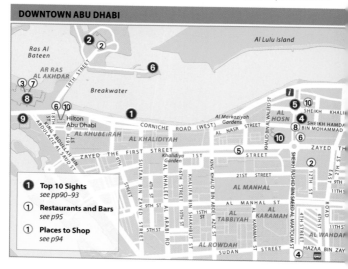

DOWNTOWN ABU DHABI

①	Top 10 Sights
	see pp90–93
①	Restaurants and Bars
	see p95
①	Places to Shop
	see p94

Previous pages Bird's-eye view of Downtown Dubai from the Burj Khalifa

Looking across the water to Al Maryah Island and its new developments

2 Marina Mall
MAP P1 ■ The Breakwater
■ 02 681 8300 ■ Open 10am–10pm,
(till midnight Thu & Fri) ■ www.marina
mall.ae

Despite its slightly out-of-the way location, the sprawling Marina Mall is one of the city's largest and most popular shopping destinations, with shops laid out between an attractive sequence of circular atriums topped with tent-shaped roofs. The highlight of the complex is the slender Marina Sky Tower, at the back of the mall, which offers superb views over the city and Corniche from the Colombiano coffee shop (floor 41) or the Tiara revolving restaurant (floor 42).

3 Al Maryah Island
MAP T3

On the northern side of Downtown, this island is the site of arguably the city's most ambitious mega-project. Planned as Abu Dhabi's new financial and business district, much of the development has yet to take shape, although the Abu Dhabi Global Market Square gives a taste of things to come, with its huge skyscrapers and chic Galleria mall (see p94).

4 World Trade Center
MAP R2 ■ Hamdan Bin
Mohammed St ■ www.wtcad.ae

One of the largest developments in Abu Dhabi, the World Trade Center is topped by the Trust Tower and the Burj Mohammed bin Rashid. The main attraction is its souk (see p94), offering a kind of Postmodern re-imagination of the traditional Arabian souk.

The soaring World Trade Center

5 Al Ittihad Square
MAP R1

A crop of supersized sculptures stand in the small park at the centre of Al Ittihad Square, creating a whimsical contrast to the surrounding tower blocks. The five sculptures feature a gigantic coffeepot, a huge perfume bottle, an elaborate plate cover, a colossal cannon and a small fort.

Potter at Abu Dhabi Heritage Village

6 Abu Dhabi Heritage Village
MAP P1 ▪ The Breakwater ▪ 02 681 4455 ▪ Open 9am–5pm Sat–Thu, 3:30–9pm Fri ▪ www.visitabudhabi.ae

For a taste of life as it was in the city before the discovery of oil, Abu Dhabi's Heritage Village is the place to come. In a superb location directly over the water from the soaring towers of the Corniche, the village comprises a line of traditional *barasti* (palm-frond) huts, some of them turned into workshops in which resident craftspeople can sometimes be seen at work.

THE DISCOVERY OF OIL

The Japanese invention of the cultured pearl and the subsequent collapse of the Gulf's pearl industry led to the granting of petroleum concessions by Sheikh Shakhbut bin Sultan Al Nahyan in 1939. It turned out to be a very wise move. The discovery of oil in 1958 and its export from 1962 made Abu Dhabi an extremely rich city.

7 Al Mina Souks
MAP T1 ▪ Open 5am–11pm

Stretching away on the northern side of Downtown Abu Dhabi is the city's Al Mina port area, stacked with cranes and busy with boats. A trio of small markets can be found here. The so-called Carpet Souk *(see p94)* comprises a small square with low-key shops. The nearby food souk is the heart of the city's retail trade in vegetables and fruit, while opposite is the lively fish market, with the day's catch laid out along the quay.

8 Emirates Palace

Abu Dhabi's magnificent pink palace hotel dominates the western end of the splendid Corniche. The majestic multi-domed exterior is surpassed in extravagance only by the dazzling interior, glittering with gold and sparkling with Swarovski crystals. The Emirates Palace was constructed to provide opulent accommodation fitting for the capital's visiting dignitaries *(see pp30–31)*.

Iconic facade of the Emirates Palace

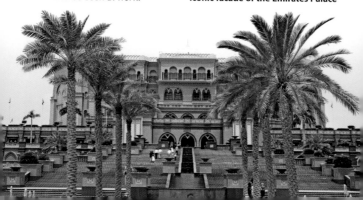

9 Etihad Towers
MAP N2 ■ Observation deck at 300: Open 10am–6pm ■ Adm ■ www.etihadtowers.com

Dominating the southwestern end of the Corniche is the huge Etihad Towers development, a cluster of five glistening skyscrapers with gently curved outlines and a gleaming metallic shine. There are superlative views over Abu Dhabi from the 74th-floor Observation Deck at 300 (in tower two) and from Ray's Bar on the 62nd floor of the Jumeirah at Etihad Towers hotel *(see p115)*.

Etihad Towers dominating the skyline

10 Qasr al Hosn
MAP R2 ■ Al Nasr St (5th St)

Located at the heart of Downtown, Qasr al Hosn (the Palace Fort) offers an unexpected throwback to earlier times. This is the oldest building in Abu Dhabi, first established back in the 1760s, after which it served as home to the ruling Al Nahyan family for the next two centuries. Most of what you see now – a high white wall dotted with a sequence of circular battlemented towers – was built in the 1940s. The fort is currently undergoing extensive renovations and will eventually reopen as a new museum showcasing the city's history, although the date is unknown.

A CORNICHE AND CITY WALK

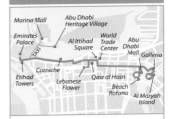

▶ **MORNING**

Start with a stroll around the stunning new Abu Dhabi Global Market Square (Sowwah Square) on **Al Maryah Island** *(see p91)* and a wander through the boutique shops of the **Galleria** *(see p94)*. Afterwards, head along the waterfront before crossing the bridge to the Downtown area. Wander past the **Abu Dhabi Mall** *(see p94)* and along 5th St, one of the city's liveliest shopping areas, then have a look into the souk at the **World Trade Center** *(see p91)* and admire the quirky statues in **Al Ittihad Square**. From here it's a short stroll past **Qasr al Hosn** to the **Lebanese Flower** restaurant *(see p95)*, where you can break for lunch.

AFTERNOON

Walk down past Al Markaziyah Gardens to the spectacular **Corniche** *(see p90)* and then take a stroll along a bit of the waterfront before jumping in a cab and heading past the **Etihad Towers** for afternoon tea in the opulent surroundings of the **Emirates Palace** hotel. Catch another cab for the short drive to the **Abu Dhabi Heritage Village**, after which you can watch the sun set from the top of the Sky Tower in the **Marina Mall** *(see p91)*.

Catch a taxi back to Downtown and enjoy the spectacular nighttime view of Al Maryah Island from the terrace of the fashionable **Finz** restaurant at the **Beach Rotana** hotel *(see p116)*. End the day with a drink at the hotel's German-themed Brauhaus pub.

See map on pp90–91 ←

Places to Shop

1 Abu Dhabi Mall
MAP T2 ■ Tourist Club area ■ 02 645 4858 ■ Open 10am–10pm (till 11pm Thu–Fri) ■ www.abudhabi mall.com

Known as "AD Mall", this popular spot has all the top-name shops.

A water feature at Marina Mall

2 Marina Mall
This enormous mall is packed with stores, cinemas and cafés. There is even an ice rink (see p91).

3 Carpet Souk
MAP U2 ■ Mina (Port) Rd

This souk is more about the buying experience than the items on offer (carpets, rugs, kilims and cushions).

4 Al Wahda Mall
MAP R3 ■ Near Central Bus Stop ■ 02 443 7000 ■ Open 10am–10pm (till 11pm Thu–Sat) ■ www.alwahda-mall.com

With more than 250 stores and a cinema hall, this recently expanded mall is now the largest in Abu Dhabi.

5 Iranian Souq
MAP U2 ■ Mina (Port) Rd

Amid the plastic items and plants sold here, you'll find Iranian painted crafts.

6 Fotouh Al Khair Centre
MAP R2 ■ Near Etisalat, opposite Cultural Foundation ■ Open 10am–10pm ■ 02 622 2241

Expats love this bright mini mall. It is home to Marks & Spencer and a number of other popular UK brands.

7 Khalifa Centre
MAP T2 ■ Tenth St, opposite Abu Dhabi Mall, Tourist Club area ■ Open 10am–1pm & 4–10pm Sat–Fri ■ 02 667 9900

Bargain here for exquisite Persian rugs, sheeshas, tribal kilims and even silver prayer boxes.

8 Hamdan St
MAP R2 ■ Sheikh Hamdan bin Mohammed St (Hamdan St)

This street sells pretty much everything. It has jewellery stores and Arabic and Bollywood music shops, as well as discount supermarkets.

9 The Galleria
MAP T2 ■ Al Maryah Island ■ Open 10am–10pm (till midnight Thu–Fri) ■ 02 616 6999

Spanning three floors, the Galleria houses numerous luxury boutique stores from across the world.

10 World Trade Center Souk
MAP R2 ■ Off Al Ittihad Square ■ 02 810 7814 ■ Open 10am–10pm (till 11pm Thu–Fri) ■ www.wtcad.ae

Explore the great selection of craft and souvenir shops at this stunning souk within the World Trade Center (see p91). There are also shops selling local food, spices and honey.

The World Trade Center Souk

Restaurants and Bars

PRICE CATEGORIES

For a three-course meal for one with half a bottle of wine (or equivalent meal), taxes and extra charges.

D Under AED 100 **DD** AED 100–400
DDD Over AED 400

1 Hanoi
MAP N2 ▪ Khalifa Bin Zayed St ▪ 02 626 1112 ▪ Open 10:30am–10:30pm daily ▪ D

The capital's original Vietnamese restaurant, this place serves classic unpretentious dishes.

2 Beijing
MAP N2 ▪ Madinat Zayed ▪ 02 621 0708 ▪ Open 11am–midnight daily ▪ D

Authentic Chinese food need not be expensive, as this popular spot pulls out all the stops to prove.

3 Hakkasan
MAP N6 ▪ Emirates Palace Hotel, Corniche West St ▪ 02 690 7999 ▪ Open 6pm–midnight daily & noon–3pm Fri–Sat ▪ DDD

This award-winning Chinese eatery serves up exquisite Cantonese staples. The opulent surroundings were designed by French interior designers Gilles & Boissier.

4 Cristal Cigar and Champagne Bar
MAP S1 ▪ Millennium Hotel, Khalifa St ▪ 02 614 6000 ▪ Open 5pm–2am daily

For a sophisticated evening, stop by this gentlemen's club-style bar for a glass of bubbly or a cigar.

5 Lebanese Flower
MAP P3 ▪ Near Choitrams Supermarket, cnr Hamdan & Fourth St, Khalidya ▪ 02 665 8700 ▪ Open 7am–3am daily ▪ No alcohol ▪ D

A must-visit restaurant serving scrumptious mezze (Arabic appetizers such as hommous and vine leaves), smoky mixed grilled meat plates and honey-soaked baklava.

6 Vasco's
MAP N2 ▪ Hilton Abu Dhabi, Corniche Rd West ▪ 02 681 1900 ▪ Open noon–3:30pm & 7pm–11pm ▪ DDD

A smart restaurant offering an incredible blend of European cooking with a pinch of Asia.

Sayad, with views to the sea

7 Sayad
MAP N1 ▪ Emirates Palace Hotel, Corniche Rd West ▪ 02 690 7999 ▪ Open 6:30–11:30pm daily ▪ DDD

Expect playful decor and fine seafood cuisine at this swanky restaurant.

8 Royal Orchid
MAP T2 ▪ Al Salam St ▪ 02 677 9911 ▪ Open noon–11:30pm ▪ No alcohol ▪ D

An authentic little Thai restaurant with a great atmosphere.

9 India Palace
MAP T2 ▪ Al Salam St ▪ 02 644 8777 ▪ Open noon–midnight daily ▪ No alcohol ▪ D

Dine on North Indian cuisine in an opulent Anglo-Indian-style setting.

10 Jazz Bar & Dining
MAP P6 ▪ Hilton Abu Dhabi, Corniche Rd West ▪ 02 681 1900 ▪ Open 7pm–2am Sun–Wed, 7pm–3am Thu & Fri

Enjoy live jazz and great cocktails at this Art Deco-inspired bar.

See map on pp90–91

██ Beyond the Centre of Abu Dhabi

Car at Ferrari World

Beyond the central Downtown area, Abu Dhabi is booming. Much of the city's ongoing future development plans are focused on Saadiyat Island, a couple of miles east from the centre. Already home to the almost-finished Abu Dhabi Louvre (a sister museum to the Louvre in Paris), the island is planned to become a key tourist destination with world-class museums, heritage sites and leisure attractions. Past here, adjacent Yas Island is where you will find the city's famous Formula 1 racetrack and swanky Yas Marina, with the vast Ferrari World and Yas Waterworld theme parks close by. Back towards the centre, the city shows its more traditional face at the vast white Sheikh Zayed Mosque, one of the world's most spectacular modern mosques.

BEYOND THE CENTRE OF ABU DHABI

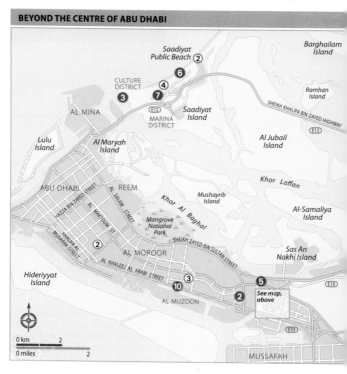

1 Bain al Jessrain
MAP V4 ■ Souk Qaryat al Beri:
Open Sat–Thu 10am–10pm, Fri 4–
10pm ■ www.soukqaryatalberi.com

Most of Abu Dhabi is actually built
on an island separated from the
mainland by a narrow sea inlet
known as Maqta Creek – it wasn't
until the opening of Maqta Bridge in
1966 that the island and mainland
were connected. Three bridges
now span the creek, whose shores
now feature several top hotels and
some of the city's most valuable real
estate. The area on the mainland
side, known as Bain al Jessrain
(Between the Bridges), is also
where you'll find the little Souk
Qaryat al Beri, which is home to a
string of boutique and eating outlets
set over two levels. Following a
Venetian theme, canals meander
throughout the pretty souk.

The striking Sheikh Zayed Mosque

1 Bain al Jessrain
(Between the Bridges)

Abu Dhabi Creek

ABU DHABI
AL AIN RD

⑤

⑦

AL MAQTA

⑨ Souk Qaryat
al Beri

KHOR AL
MAQTA'A

Shangri-La Hotel

①③⑥⑦⑧

AL KHALEEJ
AL ARABI ST

0 meters   800

0 yards   800

E10

Zeraa
Island

Yas Island

④   ⑧

④⑤⑩⑩ Yas Viceroy Hotel

E12

①⑧ Yas Marina
YAS
PLAZA ⑥⑨

⑨

**Abu Dhabi
International** ✈

MASDAR CITY

MADINAT
KHALIFA

AIRPORT RD   E20

①	**Top 10 Sights** see pp97–9
①	**Restaurants** see p100
①	**Bars** see p101

2 Sheikh Zayed Mosque
This impressive structure is
an imposing sight on the drive from
Dubai to Abu Dhabi. The mosque
is named after Sheikh Zayed bin
Sultan Al Nahyan, the founder and
the first president of the United
Arab Emirates, who is also buried
here. The building is open to non-
Muslims, but visitors should dress
conservatively (see pp28–9).

3 Abu Dhabi Louvre
MAP V2 ■ Cultural District,
Abu Dhabi ■ Adm ■ www.louvre-
abudhabi.ae

A new branch of the famous Parisian
museum, the Abu Dhabi Louvre is
the centrepiece of the huge Saadiyat
Island project, intended to form a
dedicated cultural and leisure
destination within the city, with further
museums, malls and beaches
planned. Due to open in 2017, the
building was designed by French
architect Jean Nouvel and resembles
an enormous white flying saucer
under an intricately latticed roof.
The museum will host a range of
exhibits from the Louvre's collections,
including a strong selection of
Middle Eastern and Islamic art.

Pure white sand and turquoise-blue sea at Saadiyat Public Beach

(4) Yas Waterworld

MAP W4 ■ Yas Island ■ 02 414 2000 ■ Open 10am–7pm ■ Adm; under 3s free ■ www.yaswaterworld.com

Rivalling Wild Wadi (see p78) and Aquaventure (see p84) in Dubai, Abu Dhabi's state-of-the-art water park offers more than 40 stomach-churning rides and slides, plus gentler water-based fun for kids and adults alike. Adrenaline junkies should head for the near-vertical Jebel Drop water slide. If you want to enjoy the sea itself, the nearby Yas Public Beach has loads of sand, an infinity pool and lovely loungers to relax on.

A jumble of slides, Yas Waterworld

(5) Al Maqtaa Fort

MAP V4 ■ Al Maqtaa bridge, on the right coming from Dubai

This quaint little 200-year-old fort once guarded the main approach to the city and still stands sentinel beside Al Maqtaa Bridge. The sand-coloured exterior is adorned with carved wooden doors and shuttered windows, with narrow slits above for rifles.

(6) Saadiyat Public Beach

MAP V2 ■ Open 8am–sunset ■ Adm with lounger and umbrella

This beautiful beach offers a nice change of pace from the city centre, with a huge expanse of fine white sand. The dunes behind the beach are a nesting site for turtles and a refuge for other rare flora and fauna, while dolphins are sometimes spotted offshore here. The facilities include toilets, showers and a café.

(7) Manarat al Saadiyat

MAP V2 ■ Sheikh Khalifa Hwy ■ Open 9am–8pm ■ 02 657 5800 ■ www.saadiyatculturaldistrict.ae

Great things are planned for Saadiyat Island, although it's likely to be quite a few years before the development really gets going. In the meantime, a sense of the enormous ambitions of this project-in-progress can be gleaned from a visit to Manarat al Saadiyat, hosting tantalising architectural models and other exhibits on the future island. The striking metallic building next door is the UAE Pavilion, designed by Foster + Partners for the Shanghai World Expo in 2010.

(8) Ferrari World

MAP W4 ■ Yas Island ■ 02 496 8000 ■ Open 11am–8pm (till 10pm Thu–Sat) ■ Adm; under 3s free ■ www.ferrariworldabudhabi.com

The ultimate shrine to one of the world's most famous cars – appropriate enough in a city built almost entirely using petrodollars. Billing itself as the "world's largest indoor theme park" this vast red extravaganza boasts an amazing range of rides. Highlights include a Formula 1 simulator, the world's fastest rollercoaster and the vertiginous Tower of Speed ride.

9 Aldar HQ
MAP W4 ■ Al Raha, next to the Dubai–Abu Dhabi highway

The Aldar HQ is another strong contender for the title of Abu Dhabi's most unusual building, clearly visible from the main highway as you approach from Dubai. Claimed to be the world's first circular skyscraper, the structure looks a lot like a huge magnifying glass, supported by a diagonal grid of steel girders. Casual visitors are welcome to go inside for a look at the airy atrium.

10 Capital Gate
MAP U3 ■ Al Khaleej al Arabi St

The so-called "Leaning Tower of Abu Dhabi", Capital Gate is one of the most remarkable of Abu Dhabi's many strange modern buildings. Officially recognized by Guinness World Records as the world's most tilted tower, this enormous skyscraper looks as if it's on the point of toppling headfirst into the sea, with four times more lean than even the famously wonky Leaning Tower of Pisa.

The tilting Capital Gate

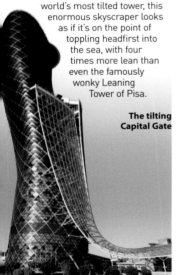

A DAY AROUND ABU DHABI

▶ MORNING

Spend the morning exploring the myriad treasures of the **Abu Dhabi Louvre** (see p97), including a large selection of Middle Eastern and Islamic art. Afterwards, pop into the nearby **Manarat al Saadiyat** exhibition to see what the future of Abu Dhabi looks like. If museums aren't your thing, spend some time on the sands at **Saadiyat Public Beach** or brave the looping rides and slides of **Yas Waterworld**. Pick up some lunch either in the museum or at one of the numerous places to eat around the **Yas Marina**.

AFTERNOON

Next, head back to the mainland. If you have time, make a short detour to see the innovative **Aldar HQ** building en route. Spend the rest of the afternoon visiting the iconic **Sheikh Zayed Mosque** and admiring its incredibly ornate courtyard and interior.

As evening approaches, catch a cab for the short drive over to **Bain al Jessrain**. Look out for the 200-year-old **Al Maqtaa Fort** and then dive into **Qaryat al Beri** souk to explore the boutiques and eateries there. Watch the sun go down over the historic Maqtaa Creek whilst sipping a cocktail at the kitsch **Left Bank** (see p100). Afterwards, head to one of the many excellent restaurants in the area. **Bord Eau** (see p101) at the Shangri La Hotel is an especially memorable place for a romantic evening meal, boasting sweeping views across the creek from the terrace.

See map on pp96–7 ←

Bars

Y Bar, with its striking brick-vaulted ceiling

1 Y Bar
MAP W4 ▪ Yas Island Rotana Hotel ▪ 02 656 4000 ▪ Open noon–2am ▪ www.rotana.com

A funky bar with an outdoor terrace. It's a great place for evening cocktails.

2 Cabana 9, Saadiyat Beach Club
MAP V2 ▪ Saadiyat Island ▪ 02 656 3500 ▪ Open 8am–10pm ▪ www.saadiyatbeachclub.ae

Sip a drink overlooking the sea at this idyllic beachfront pool bar.

3 Relax@12
MAP V3 ▪ Aloft Hotel, Khaleej al Arabi St ▪ 02 654 5138 ▪ Open 5pm till late ▪ www.relaxat12abudhabi.com

A cool rooftop bar offering sweeping views through huge picture windows. Visiting DJs keep things lively.

4 Turquoiz
MAP V2 ▪ The St. Regis Saadiyat Island Resort ▪ 02 498 8888 ▪ Open noon–11pm Sun–Thu, noon–2am Fri & Sat ▪ www.turquoizabudhabi.com

A beach restaurant offering an array of appetizing seafood, light meals, delicious snacks and signature cocktails.

5 Chameleon
MAP V4 ▪ Fairmont Bab Al Bahr, Bain Al Jessrain ▪ 02 654 3238 ▪ Open 6pm–1am Tue–Sun

This chic cocktail bar with views over the water is one of the classiest spots in the city. Prices reflect its popularity.

6 Stars 'N' Bars
MAP W4 ▪ Yas Island, Abu Dhabi ▪ 02 565 0101 ▪ Open 11:30am–2am daily

Enjoy a variety of international cuisine along with free arcade games at this American-style sports bar.

7 Sorso
MAP V4 ▪ Ritz Carlton ▪ 02 818 8282 ▪ Open 5pm–1am ▪ www.ritzcarlton.com

A smart bar that looks like the lounge of an old-school European gentlemen's club, with huge armchairs and plush sofas.

8 Belgian Beer Café
MAP W4 ▪ Radisson Blu Hotel, Yas Island ▪ 02 656 2407 ▪ Open noon–2am Sat–Wed, noon–3am Thu & Fri

A chic café serving lunch and dinner favourites accompanied by a fine selection of Belgian beverages.

9 Iris
MAP W4 ▪ Yas Marina ▪ 055 160 5636 ▪ Open 6pm–3am Mon–Sat ▪ www.irisabudhabi.com

Pose with a drink at this chic bar-club, while admiring views of Yas Marina.

10 Skylite Rooftop Lounge
MAP W4 ▪ Yas Viceroy Hotel, Yas Island ▪ 02 656 0600 ▪ Open 6pm–1am (8pm–2am May–Sept) ▪ www.viceroyhotelsandresorts.com

A hip venue set under a dramatic latticed roof, with a nightly DJ.

See map on pp96–7

Restaurants

1 Bord Eau
MAP V4 ■ Shangri-La Hotel, Qaryat Al Beri ■ 02 509 8888 ■ Open 6:30–11:30pm ■ DDD

This elegant French restaurant in the Shangri-La Hotel offers classic French dishes and modern, innovative cuisine. There is also a really excellent wine list.

2 Sardinia
MAP U3 ■ Abu Dhabi Country Club ■ 02 657 7640 ■ Open noon–3pm & 7–11pm ■ DD

An award-winning kitchen serving top-notch international cuisine. A complimentary amuse-bouche is served between each course.

3 Entrecôte Café de Paris
MAP V4 ■ Shangri-La Hotel, Souk Qaryat al Beri ■ 02 557 6508 ■ Open noon–midnight ■ DD

An offshoot of the famous Geneva restaurant, serving just a single dish – the famed entrecôte fillet steak – in the café's special secret sauce.

4 Amici
MAP W4 ■ Yas Viceroy Hotel, Yas Island ■ 02 656 0600 ■ Open 12:30–3pm & 7–11pm ■ DD

An Italian restaurant serving authentic freshly made pasta and wood-fired pizza, plus good antipasti.

5 Atayeb
MAP W4 ■ Yas Viceroy Hotel, Yas Island ■ 02 656 0600 ■ 7pm–1am Sun–Fri ■ DD

This intimate restaurant (with a spectacular outdoor terrace) offers a rich array of classic Levantine dishes from Lebanon and Syria, cooked over charcoal stoves.

6 Hoi An
MAP V4 ■ Shangri-La Hotel, Qaryat Al Beri ■ 02 509 8555 ■ Open 6–11:30pm ■ DD

A smart colonial-style restaurant dishing up great Vietnamese cuisine.

PRICE CATEGORIES

For a three-course meal for one with half a bottle of wine (or equivalent meal), taxes and extra charges.

D Under AED 100 ■ DD AED 100–400
DDD Over AED 400

7 Shang Palace
MAP V4 ■ Shangri-La Hotel, Qaryat Al Beri ■ 02 509 8555 ■ Open noon–3pm & 7–11:30pm ■ DD

Enjoy excellent Chinese cuisine cooked with panache.

8 p&c by Sergi Arola
MAP V4 ■ Shangri-La Hotel, Qaryat Al Beri ■ 02 509 8777 ■ Open 7–11:30pm ■ DD

Sip cocktails and tuck into a selection of tapas dishes at this glitzy venue overlooking Maqta Creek.

9 Ushna
MAP V4 ■ Souk Qaryat al Beri ■ 02 558 1769 ■ Open 12:30–11:00pm ■ DD

A chic North Indian restaurant in an attractive waterside setting.

10 Angar
MAP W4 ■ Yas Viceroy Hotel, Yas Island ■ 02 656 0600 ■ Open 7pm–11am Wed–Mon (from 2pm Fri) ■ DD

A stylish and upmarket restaurant serving innovative and delicately spiced modern Indian cuisine.

Interior of the sophisticated Angar

Streetsmart

Al Fahidi Metro Station, Bur Dubai

Getting To and Around Dubai and Abu Dhabi

Arriving by Air

Centrally located just outside the old city, sleek **Dubai Airport** is one of the world's best. **Emirates Airline** has its own, ultramodern terminal (3), while most other long-haul international flights land at Terminal 1.

Abu Dhabi Airport is also very modern in design and international visitors will arrive into an unusual circular terminal (1).

If you're from one of the 49 countries eligible for an on-the-spot visa (see p106), the entry process is a breeze. If you don't come from an eligible country, make sure you have your visa documents to hand. Be aware that the UEA has very strict narcotics laws, and some prescription drugs are banned. Check with your local UAE embassy before flying, as you may have to ask your doctor for documentation.

There are almost always plenty of taxis at both airports. In Dubai the fixed rate from the airport is AED 25, with a fare into Deira or Bur Dubai of around AED 50, or AED 75–100 to Jumeirah. Alternatively, Terminals 1 and 3 are both connected to the Dubai Metro. There are also various airport buses including the useful **Sky Bus (Terhab)** network, run by **RTA**, which runs 24 hours from all three airport terminals with departures every 30 minutes. This is useful if you arrive at night when the metro isn't running. To get from Abu Dhabi airport, you'll either have to catch a taxi (around AED 70–80 into the city centre) or ride the 24-hour airport bus #A1, which runs regularly into the centre (AED 4). It's around a 30–40 minute drive into the city, depending on traffic.

Arriving by Sea

Numerous cruise ships include Dubai in their itineraries, docking at the **Dubai Cruise Terminal** in Port Rashid, centrally located between Jumeirah and Bur Dubai.

Arriving by Road

The UAE's land borders with Saudi Arabia are open only to GCC nationals. There are five border crossings with Oman currently open, with visas issued on the spot to citizens of 49 different countries (see p106).

Transport Tickets

Run by RTA, almost all public transport in Dubai, including the metro, tram and city buses, is covered by the **Nol** ticketing system. You'll need a ticket before you use any of these since none are sold onboard any form of transport. The cheapest option is the reusable Nol Red Ticket (AED 2). To use this you need to pre-pay the correct fare for each journey you make. You can also use it to buy a one-day travel pass (AED 20), offering unlimited transport around the city. There are also three types of rechargeable Nol cards (Silver, Gold and Blue) which can be pre-loaded with up to AED 500 of credit. Cards/tickets can be bought and topped up at any metro station and various other locations. Fares are identical across metro, tram and bus networks, and offer superb value, costing between AED 3 and AED 7.5 (or double that in the more luxurious metro/tram Gold Class compartments).

By Metro

The impressive driverless **Dubai Metro** is by far the quickest and cheapest way to get around. There are two lines – Red and Green – which between them cover most of the city's sights. Trains run daily from around 5:30am to midnight (later on Thursday) and from 10am on Friday. There are departures every five to ten minutes. Children under five or shorter than 0.9m travel free. All trains have a plusher and more expensive Gold Class compartment and a dedicated carriage for women and children.

By Tram

Opened in 2014, the superb **Dubai Tram** loops around the marina and continues up the coast for several kilometres, providing access to places the metro doesn't reach. The system connects directly to the metro and also links to the Palm Monorail *(see p85)*. Trams run Saturday to Thursday 6:30am–1am and Friday 9am–1am, with services every 8 minutes.

By Bus

Dubai Buses, run by RTA, has an extensive bus network, although services tend to cover routes and areas of little interest to most visitors. Abu Dhabi buses **(DoT)** are more useful, with various routes criss-crossing Downtown. Fares are around AED 3–4 per journey. There are also regular bus services between the two cities, and to other major destinations across the country.

By Taxi

Taxis are a great and affordable way of getting around in both Dubai and Abu Dhabi. Vehicles can be hailed anywhere on the street, and there are taxi ranks at most shopping malls – though during busy times it might be better to call ahead. All taxis use meters and cost around AED 1.5 per km plus flag fall. In Dubai the flag fall is AED 5, with a minimum charge of AED 12 per ride. In Abu Dhabi the flag fare is AED 3.50 (AED 4 at night; minimum fare AED 10dh from 10pm to 6am). Reputable companies are the **Dubai Taxi Corporation** and **TransAD** (for Abu Dhabi).

By Car

Driving in Dubai can be challenging, given the sometimes heavy traffic, labyrinthine road layouts and often aggressive driving styles, but is feasible if you're confident behind the wheel. Cars drive on the right, and speed limits are 60km/h on city streets, 80km/h on major city roads, and 100–120km/h on highways. Do not drink and drive unless you want to spend the night (or longer) in jail.

There are car-rental desks at airports, hotels and other locations. The international companies **Avis**, **Budget**, **Europcar** and **Hertz** are all well represented.

By Boat

The plush **Dubai Ferry** runs three times daily between Bur Dubai and Dubai Marina (75 minutes), and there are also various sightseeing round trips. Fares on all trips are AED 50. In the old city, *abras* criss-cross Dubai Creek, connecting Deira and Bur Dubai. The fare is AED 1 per person. You can also hire your own *abra* to cruise the creek for AED 120 per hour.

By Foot

Neither Dubai nor Abu Dhabi is very pedestrian friendly, apart from Dubai's souks, marinas and Al Fahidi, and the Corniche in Abu Dhabi. Elsewhere, be cautious on pedestrian crossings, which drivers ignore.

DIRECTORY

ARRIVING BY AIR

Abu Dhabi Airport
ⓦ abudhabiairport.ae

Dubai Airport
ⓦ dubaiairport.com

Emirates Airline
ⓦ emirates.com

Sky Bus (Terhab)
ⓦ dubai-buses.com

ARRIVING BY SEA

Dubai Cruise Terminal
ⓦ dubaicruiseterminal.com

TRANSPORT TICKETS

Nol ⓦ nol.ae

BY METRO

Dubai Metro
ⓦ dubai-metro.me

BY TRAM

Dubai Tram
ⓦ alsufouhtram.com

BY BUS

DoT
ⓦ dot.abudhabi.ae

RTA
ⓦ dubai-buses.com

BY TAXI

Dubai Taxi Corporation
ⓦ dubaitaxi.ae

TransAD
ⓦ transad.ae

BY CAR

Avis
ⓦ avis.com

Budget
ⓦ budget-uae.com

Europcar
ⓦ europcardubai.com
ⓦ europcar-abudhabi.com

Hertz
ⓦ hertzuae.com

BY BOAT

Dubai Ferry
ⓦ dubai-ferry.com

Practical Information

Passports and Visas

Free 30-day (90-day for some nationalities) visit visas are available on arrival to citizens from 47 countries. Passports must be valid for six months from the date of entry to the UAE. Visas for 30 days (but not for 90 days) can be extended by the **General Directorate of Residency and Foreigners Affairs** at a cost of AED 620.

Customs Regulations

The duty-free allowance for each traveller is 400 cigarettes, 500g of tobacco, 50 cigars and 4 litres of alcohol. It's not possible to buy alcohol in shops in the UAE without a liquor license (only available to UAE residents), so buy duty free at the airport if you want to have your own supply. In addition to the usual items (firearms, illegal drugs and pornography), it is forbidden to bring in any banned movies, TV programs and offensive publications, especially films and programs that may include scenes with passionate kissing, sex, nudity or semi-nudity, or drugs use. Goods made in Israel (or bearing Israeli logos) are also forbidden. Check the **Dubai Customs** website for the most up-to-date information.

Travel Safety Advice

Visitors can get up-to-date travel safety information from the **US Department of State**, from the **Australian Department of Foreign Affairs and Trade**, and from the **UK Foreign and Commonwealth Office**.

Embassies and Consulates

Canada, the **UK**, the **US**, and other countries have consular representation in the region. Check your consulate's UAE website for travel warnings and security information.

Travel Insurance

While petty crime is rare in the UAE, insurance covering loss of luggage and theft is always good to have, along with comprehensive health and dental insurance. Hospitals are very efficient, but services are expensive.

Health

No special vaccinations are needed for the UAE. The biggest danger to your health is the heat. Take precautions to avoid dehydration, sunburn and sunstroke. Be careful, too, when crossing roads, and when driving. Tap water is safe to drink. At most, you may experience an upset tummy as your body adjusts to new bacteria. If you need urgent medical attention, call the **Emergency Number**.

Standards are outstanding in both private and public hospitals, although the service is faster at emergency departments at private hospitals. Good hospitals for tourists include the **American Hospital** and **Emirates Hospital** in Dubai, and the **Burjeel Hospital** and **Cleveland Clinic** in Abu Dhabi.

The UAE also has good dentists and consultations are reasonably priced. In an emergency, the best place to go is the **British Dental Clinic** (branches in Dubai and Abu Dhabi).

There are numerous pharmacies, including many that open 24 hours (ask at your hotel for the nearest branch).

Personal Security

While petty crime is almost unheard of, be sensible – don't leave valuables unattended and don't flash cash around. As a pedestrian be vigilant; drivers will not stop for you on a crossing, so cross only at lights where possible. If your taxi driver is driving too fast or recklessly, tell him to slow down ("shway shway").

If you're driving and you have an accident, first get out of harm's way, then call the police for instructions. Do not move the car unless instructed to do so by the police. Rainy weather makes driving hazardous simply because UAE residents aren't used to driving in the rain – they won't necessarily slow down. Decelerate or pull over in sand storms when visibility is poor. When you see oncoming drivers with their hazard lights on, it means conditions are even worse up ahead.

The UAE is an Islamic state and you can land in trouble for not respecting local religious customs and decency laws. Never drink alcohol and drive. In Dubai and Abu Dhabi, arrests have resulted from foreigners being too affectionate in public. If you get arrested, do not sign anything in Arabic immediately. Your consulate should be your first call – they can help facilitate contact with a local bilingual lawyer.

In Sharjah, it's illegal for women to travel in a vehicle with men other than their husband. Women must dress modestly and not show their upper arms or back.

Women travelling solo in the UAE shouldn't experience any harassment if they follow local norms. Sit in the back seat of taxis and in the "women's section" of buses. Dedicated women's queues at banks and government departments indicate that women will get preferential service.

Do not attempt to bring medicinal drugs into the country. Bear in mind that even some prescription drugs, such as codeine, and anti-depressant and HRT medications, are banned. The UAE has a zero tolerance policy on recreational drugs. Penalties and sentences are harsh. While the death penalty is an option, it's rarely applied.

Homosexuality is illegal and punishable with harsh penalties, although rarely enforced. You will sometimes see men from Central Asia and the Indian Subcontinent holding hands – this signifies friendship. You'll also see Emirati men rub noses when they meet, in the same way that close male friends kiss cheeks in Europe's Mediterranean countries.

When swimming, take warning signs about dangerous rips and strong undertows seriously. Despite the calm appearance of the water, Dubai's beaches have very powerful undercurrents.

In Dubai, if you leave something behind in a taxi, you'll need to file a report at **Dubai Taxi**. For any other lost property, contact the **Police Lost and Found**.

Casual irritations while visiting Dubai include the numerous touts in old city souks attempting to sell "copy watches", "copy bags" and so on. Male visitors may also be approached by prostitutes in bars, especially in the older parts of the city.

DIRECTORY

PASSPORTS AND VISAS

General Directorate of Residency and Foreigners Affairs
☎ 04 313 9999, 800 5111
🖥 dnrd.ae

CUSTOMS REGULATIONS

Dubai Customs
🖥 dubaicustoms.gov.ae

TRAVEL SAFETY ADVICE

Australian Department of Foreign Affairs and Trade
🖥 dfat.gov.au
🖥 smartraveller.gov.au

UK Foreign and Commonwealth Office
🖥 gov.uk/foreign-travel-advice

US Department of State
🖥 travel.state.gov

EMBASSIES AND CONSULATES

Canada
🖥 canadainternational.gc.ca

UK
🖥 ukinuae.fco.gov.uk/en

US
🖥 dubai.usconsulate.gov
🖥 abudhabi.usembassy.gov

HEALTH

American Hospital (Dubai)
☎ 04 337 5000
🖥 ahdubai.com

British Dental Clinic
☎ 04 342 1318 (Dubai)
☎ 02 677 3308 (Abu Dhabi)
🖥 britishdentalclinic.com

Burjeel Hospital (Abu Dhabi)
☎ 04 313 9999, 800 5111
02 508 5555
🖥 burjeel.com

Cleveland Clinic (Abu Dhabi)
☎ 04 313 9999, 800 5111, 800 8 2223
🖥 clevelandclinic abudhabi.ae

Emergency Number (Ambulance, Fire and Police)
☎ 999

Emirates Hospital (Dubai)
☎ 04 313 9999, 800 5111, 04 349 6666
🖥 emirateshospital.ae

PERSONAL SECURITY

Dubai Taxi
🖥 dubaitaxi.ae

Police Lost and Found
☎ 901
(Dubai)
☎ 02 699 9999
(Abu Dhabi)

Currency and Banking

The UAE's currency is the UAE dirham, written as AED (Arab Emirates Dirham) or as Dh. One dirham is divided into 100 fils. Notes are in denominations of AED 5, AED 10, AED 20, AED 50, AED 100, AED 200, AED 500 and AED 1000. Coins are available as 25 fils, 50 fils and one dirham. The UAE dirham is pegged to the US dollar. US$1 is equal to AED 3.67. All other currencies fluctuate, but at the time of writing €1 was equal to AED 4 and £1 was worth AED 5.

Numerous international banks operate in the UAE, including **HSBC**, **Citibank** and **Standard Chartered Bank**. Good local banks include **National Bank of Abu Dhabi**, **Mashreq Bank** and **National Bank of Dubai**. Globally linked ATMs are everywhere. American Express, Mastercard and Visa are widely accepted and credit cards can be used almost anywhere.

There are also numerous bureaux de change, including the leading **Al Ansari Exchange**, which has branches all over the city, including in many malls.

Telephone and Internet

To phone the UAE from abroad, dial your international access code, the UAE country code 971, then 4 for Dubai or 2 for Abu Dhabi, followed by the local number. To dial a mobile from abroad, dial 971 50/55/56 followed by the mobile number. Within the UAE, dial 050/055/056 for mobiles, 04 to call Dubai from outside the emirate and 02 to phone Abu Dhabi from another emirate.

If you're bringing your own mobile/cellphone from home, note that GSM phones (the type typically used in Europe) will work in Dubai, but make sure any international call bar is switched off. North American CDMA phones will not work, so you'll have to either bring a non-CDMA phone from home or purchase a handset locally.

If you need a mobile, it's generally easier (and cheaper) to get a local SIM card. The national telecommunications company **Etisalat** offers visitors a useful "Visitor Mobile Line" (AED 35, including 20 minutes of free local calls), which gives you a SIM card and allows you to make calls at local rates. The card is is available at the Etisalat shops and other outlets. You'll need to present your passport when buying a SIM card.

There is WiFi access everywhere. Etisalat operates numerous WiFi "hotspots" in shopping malls, restaurants, coffee shops and elswhere. You can pay online with a credit card, with rates starting at around AED 10 per hour.

Post and Couriers

Emirates Post is the UAE's national postal service. You can buy stamps at any post office and at some stationery shops. Mail to Europe, North America and Australasia takes about 10 days. It's unreliable, however, so register anything valuable or use a courier for anything urgent. Emirates Post also provides surface and air delivery services for sending large parcels, although courier services are more reliable. Companies with a good reputation for service include **Aramex**, **FedEx** and **DHL**. All will pick up from your hotel – you can pay on collection if you don't have an account.

TV, Radio and Newspapers

The UAE has a number of daily English-language newspapers (mostly AED 3–4), although all practise some degree of self-censorship in order to avoid offending the government. The best is *The National*, published in Abu Dhabi. *Gulf News* (published in Dubai) is also reasonable, while the online newspaper *Emirates 24/7* provides the latest updates.

The biggest of the various Emirati television channels is the English-language **Dubai One**, which mainly screens repackaged US shows and movies, plus a few local programmes. There are also several English-language radio stations including **Virgin Radio Dubai** (104.4 FM), though none is notably interesting.

Opening Hours

The UAE weekend is Friday and Saturday. Business hours aren't fixed but, generally, shopping malls and supermarkets are open daily 10am–10pm (sometimes later on Friday and Saturday). Shops in the streets open at approximately the same times but sometimes close for lunch from 1 to 4/5pm. Government departments open around 7am and close to the public around 3pm. Private companies usually work 9am–6pm. Museum opening hours fluctuate wildly, and some smaller places close during the afternoon.

Time Difference

The UAE time zone is GMT+4. It is 9 hours ahead of North American Eastern Standard Time, 12 hours ahead of North American Western Standard Time, and 6 hours behind Australian Eastern Standard Time. There is no daylight saving.

Electrical Appliances

UAE power sockets generally accept the UK three-prong plug operating on 220/240 volts, although you may also see the European two-round-prong plug. It's a good idea to bring an adaptor that works for both. Some hotels have adaptors you can borrow, or you can buy them in supermarkets.

Weather

The UAE has an arid desert climate with infrequent rainfall. Temperatures average 20°C (68°F) in winter to 45°C (113°F) in summer. Winter (December to January) is usually when Dubai is at its best and busiest, although you may experience a little rain and overcast skies. This is when the Dubai Shopping Festival, Global Village and most major sporting events take place. October to November and March to April are a bit hotter and are almost guaranteed sunshine. Summer (May to September) is scorching and it's almost impossible to do anything except lounge by a pool or stay in air-conditioned buildings, although hotel prices tumble dramatically. The holy month of Ramadan presents some challenges to visitors and is best avoided unless you want to experience the country's more traditional side.

Travellers with Disabilities

Developers in Dubai and Abu Dhabi have worked hard to cater for visitors with specific requirements. Most of the two cities' more modern and upmarket hotels now have specially adapted rooms, although cheaper accommodation is harder to find.

Transport facilities are also good. There are excellent services at both airports for visitors with disabilities, while the Dubai Metro boasts tactile guide paths, wheelchair spaces in compartments and other facilities. The **Special Needs Taxi** service can be booked in Dubai and in Abu Dhabi. Many of the city's malls also have some facilities, including specially adapted toilets.

DIRECTORY

CURRENCY AND BANKING

Al Ansari Exchange
W alansariexchange.com

Citibank
W citibank.ae

HSBC
W hsbc.ae

Mashreq Bank
W mashreqbank.com

National Bank of Abu Dhabi
W nbad.com

National Bank of Dubai
W emiratesnbd.co.uk

Standard Chartered Bank
W sc.com/ae

TELEPHONE AND INTERNET

Etisalat
W etisalat.ae

POST AND COURIERS

Aramex
W aramex.com

DHL
W dhl.ae

Emirates Post
W emiratespost.com

FedEx
W fedex.com/ae

TV, RADIO AND NEWSPAPERS

Dubai One
W dmi.ae/dubaione

Emirates 24/7
W emirates247.com

Gulf News
W gulfnews.com

The National
W thenational.ae

Virgin Radio Dubai
W virginradiodubai.com

TRAVELLERS WITH DISABILITIES

Special Needs Taxi
C 04 208 0808 (Dubai)
C 600 53 53 53 (Abu Dhabi)

Sources of Information

Tourism in Dubai is overseen by the **Department of Tourism and Commerce Marketing (DTCM)** and in Abu Dhabi by the **Abu Dhabi Tourism and Culture Authority (ADTCA)**. There are no proper tourist offices in either Dubai or Abu Dhabi, but both DTCM and ADTCA maintain tourist offices overseas and operate helpful websites.

For information on the latest events and happenings, the best resources are *Time Out Dubai* and *Time Out Abu Dhabi* magazines. **800Tickets** sell tickets for many major music (and other) events. *What's On* magazine is also handy.

For more detailed practical information, the government-led website **UAE Interact** is sometimes useful, as is the brilliant (though now somewhat out-of-date) expat-run **Dubai FAQs** website.

The best source of breaking local news is the website of *The National* newspaper *(see p109)*. There are also a few blogs worth browsing including **Dubai at Random** and (for food) the excellent **I Live in a Frying Pan**.

Trips and Tours

There are dozens of tour operators in both Dubai and Abu Dhabi offering a fairly stereotypical range of desert outings, trips to neighbouring cities and dinner *dhow* cruises.

Arabian Adventures *(see p33)* is the biggest and best. Hop-on hop-off sightseeing bus tours are offered by **Big Bus Tours** in both Dubai and Abu Dhabi, while the unusual **Wonderbus** *(see p54)* in Dubai is another enjoyable tour.

Abras can be chartered *(see pp16–17)* for your own private cruise up and down the creek in Dubai, and there are also sightseeing trips aboard the **Dubai Ferry**.

Walking tours of Al Fahidi are offered by **SMCCU** *(see p19)*, and interesting foodie tours of offbeat Dubai eateries by **Frying Pan Adventures**. **Shaheen Xtreme** offer falconry experiences at the Dubai Desert Conservation Reserve *(see p33)*, while for a walk on the wild side in the mountains of the UAE and Oman, contact **UAE Trekkers** or **Absolute Adventure**.

For the ultimate view of either Dubai or Abu Dhabi, try a helicopter ride with **Emirates Helicopter Tours** and **Abu Dhabi Helicopter** respectively.

Shopping

There are basically two types of shopping in Dubai and Abu Dhabi: modern malls and traditional souks. Shopping malls are every-where, from huge mega-developments to low-key local places. Many leading local and international shops have outlets in malls, and chains such as **Damas** (jewellery), **Paris Gallery** (perfume) and **Grand Stores** (electronics and cameras) can be found in almost all the major shopping centres. Prices are fixed and credit cards normally accepted.

Shopping in traditional souks of the old city is a different affair. Prices are generally lower and haggling is expected (credit cards may not be accepted except for big-ticket items). A lot of the items on sale consist of everyday essentials, but you'll also find interesting collectibles – gold, spices, perfumes, designer fakes and antiques.

Where to Eat

There's a huge range of places to eat in both Dubai and Abu Dhabi, from inexpensive local cafés to extravagant fine-dining venues overseen by Michelin-starred chefs.

There's also a huge array of cuisines on offer. This is one of the best places to sample classic dishes from across the Middle East including traditional Arabian cuisine (or "Lebanese", as it's often described), along with Iranian, Moroccan and Emirati specialities. Indian food is also popular, as is Italian and Chinese.

Cheaper places are aimed largely at Asian expats living in the city, which explains the huge number of Indian and Pakistani restaurants across the old city. There are plenty of inexpensive cafés serving up Arabian food including *shawarma* kebabs in pitta bread plus other local dishes.

More expensive places are largely found attached to hotels and come in every conceivable shape and form from opulent Arabian-themed venues to ultra-chic boltholes. Dining next to the sea is popular, and many places offer outdoor terraces – those with outdoor seating may also offer sheesha (waterpipes).

Tipping is generally not expected but is appreciated if you've enjoyed your meal and service. A 10 per cent service charge may be added to cover the tip, along with other taxes. These can add up to 25 per cent of the basic cost of a meal and drinks, so check before if included.

Children are generally well-catered for and welcome everywhere except at the very best fine-dining restaurants.

Where to Stay

There's a mind-boggling array of accommodation in both Dubai and Abu Dhabi. The vast majority in both cities is generally in large and almost exclusively modern hotels – although there are a handful of more characterful small hotels in historic houses available in Dubai, including several places run by the Heritage Collection. You'll also find plenty of Airbnb options and loads of self-catering apartments – **Golden Sands** is the main local operator, with over a dozen apartment blocks in Bur Dubai.

There is considerable variety amongst the more upmarket hotels. At the top end of the scale places range from chic modernist highrises through to lavish resorts built in opulent pseudo-Arabian style. Cheaper places, however, tend to be functional concrete boxes of rather uniform appearance. The main local chain is the luxurious, Dubai-owned **Jumeirah** group, although most of the world's leading hotel companies now have at least one establishment in each city, often several.

Accommodation is available on all the usual booking websites. Rates vary considerably from month to month (sometimes from week to week), peaking during the winter months and falling hugely during the summer *(see p109)*. During busy periods, such as the religious festival of Eid, hotel prices can soar. Rates start from around AED 250 (US$70) for a double in a rock-bottom, old-city one-star hotel, rising up into the thousands of dollars per night at top places. Many hotels quote room rates exclusive of relevant government taxes, which can bump the price up by 25 per cent – always check before booking.

DIRECTORY

SOURCES OF INFORMATION

800Tickets
W 800tickets.com

Abu Dhabi Tourism and Culture Authority (ADTCA)
W tcaabudhabi.ae

Department of Tourism and Commerce Marketing (DTCM)
W visitdubai.com/en

Dubai at Random
W dubaiatrandom.blogspot.co.uk

Dubai FAQs
W dubaifaqs.com

I Live in a Frying Pan
W iliveinafryingpan.com

Time Out Abu Dhabi
W timeoutabudhabi.com

Time Out Dubai
W timeoutdubai.com

UAE Interact
W uaeinteract.com

What's On Abu Dhabi
W whatson.ae/abudhabi

What's On Dubai
W whatson.ae/dubai

TRIPS AND TOURS

Absolute Adventure
C 04 392 6463
W adventure.ae

Abu Dhabi Helicopter
W abudhabihelicoptertour.com

Big Bus Tours
W eng.bigbustours.com/dubai
W eng.bigbustours.com/abudhabi

Dubai Ferry
W dubai-ferry.com

Emirates Helicopter Tours
W emirateshelicoptertours.com

Frying Pan Adventures
W fryingpanadventures.com

Shaheen Xtreme
W royalshaheen.ae

UAE Trekkers
W uaetrekkers.com

SHOPPING

Damas
W damasjewellery.com

Grand Stores
W www.grandstores.com

Paris Gallery
W parisgallery.com

WHERE TO STAY

Golden Sands
W goldensandsdubai.com

Jumeirah
W jumeirah.com

Places to Stay

PRICE CATEGORIES

For a standard, double room per night (with breakfast if included), taxes and extra charges.

D Under AED 600   **DD** AED 600–1500
DDD Over AED 1500

Luxury City Hotels in Dubai

Dusit Thani
MAP C6 ■ Sheikh Zayed Rd ■ 04 343 3333 ■ www.dusit.com ■ DD
What sets the Dusit apart is its gentle welcoming Thai hospitality, from the "Sawadee-ka" greeting to the Thai canapés. The spacious rooms cater well to the business traveller, but it's worth paying extra for Club Rooms.

Fairmont
MAP E5 ■ Sheikh Zayed Rd ■ 04 332 5555 ■ www.fairmont.com ■ DD
Convenient for business, shopping and sightseeing, the hotel's architecture and plush rooms ooze elegance and style.

Grosvenor House
MAP B2 ■ Dubai Marina ■ 04 399 8888 ■ www.grosvenorhouse-dubai.com ■ DD
Spacious well-appointed rooms at this swanky hotel have marina or sea views. Guests can use the beach and access water activities at its sister hotel, the Royal Meridien.

Jumeirah Emirates Towers
MAP D6 ■ Sheikh Zayed Rd ■ 04 330 0000 ■ www.jumeirahemiratestowers.com ■ DD
The city's most stylish business hotel occupies one of the two landmark Emirates Towers. The spectacular lobby is a sight in its own right, while the attached Boulevard mall has several good places to eat.

Radisson Blu Hotel
MAP L2 ■ Baniyas Rd, Deira ■ 04 222 7171 ■ www.radissonblu.com ■ DD
The oldest five-star in the city, very centrally located with comfortable rooms and lovely creek views from small balconies. The superb selection of in-house restaurants and bars is one of the best in the city.

Shangri-La
MAP C5 ■ Sheikh Zayed Rd ■ 04 343 8888 ■ www.shangri-la.com ■ DD
One of Dubai's classiest city hotels, it boasts immaculate service and beautifully furnished rooms designed in contemporary Asian style, plus several excellent in-house restaurants.

Grand Hyatt Dubai
MAP E2 ■ Al Qataiyat Rd, Bur Dubai ■ 04 317 1234 ■ www.dubai.grand.hyatt.com ■ DDD
This massive property has marvellous views over Creekside Park across to the Dubai Creek Golf and Yacht Club, but it's easy to let the myriad attractions within the hotel distract you. There's a wonderful interior rainforest garden with *dhow* bottoms embedded in the ceiling and a variety of bars and restaurants.

The Palace
MAP C6 ■ Downtown Burj Khalifa ■ 04 428 7888 ■ www.theaddress.com ■ DDD
Overlooking the Dubai Fountain, this luxurious offering is designed in lavish mock-Arabian style. Facilities include three international restaurants, a spa and excellent business facilities. Despite its close proximity to the busy Dubai Mall, a stay here still offers a calm and tranquil experience.

Park Hyatt Dubai
MAP E2 ■ Dubai Creek Golf and Yacht Club, Deira ■ 04 602 1234 ■ www.dubai.park.hyatt.com ■ DDD
This beautiful white Moroccan-inspired low-rise hotel is situated on one of the most sublime spots on Dubai creek, offering guests idyllic views over the marina and yacht club.

Raffles Dubai
MAP H6 ■ Sheikh Rashis Rd ■ 04 324 8888 ■ www.raffles.com ■ DDD
The Middle East's first Raffles combines warmth and luxury with impeccable service. Its enormous rooms have great views from the distinctive Egyptian-style pyramid building, which gels with the nearby Wafi shopping complex.

Luxury Beach Hotels in Dubai

Jumeirah Beach Hotel

MAP C2 ■ Jumeirah Rd ■ 04 348 0000 ■ www. jumeirahbeachhotel.com ■ DD

While the interiors of this wave-shaped hotel are rather gaudy when compared with Dubai's chic new hotels, families are still very enthusiastic about the bright, bold colours, excellent beach facilities and innumerable kids' activities.

Le Meridien Mina Seyahi Resort

MAP B2 ■ Al Sufouh Rd, Jumeirah, Dubai ■ 04 399 3333 ■ www.lemeridien-minaseyahi.com ■ DD

This dated resort hotel is nothing much to look at but boasts one of Dubai's best stretches of beachfront, backed by splendid palm-studded gardens dotted with several swimming pools. Rates are generally lower than in nearby places, making this one of the most affordable of the marina resorts.

Westin Mina Seyahi

MAP B2 ■ Al Sufouh Rd, Dubai Marina ■ 04 399 4141 ■ www. westinminaseyahi.com ■ DD

This elegant addition to Dubai's five-star coastline boasts spectacular views over the Arabian Gulf. The beautifully appointed rooms are spacious and well-equipped; some, but not all, have balconies. Other facilities include a spa, gym, several bars and restaurants, and excellent water sports.

Al Qasr

MAP C2 ■ Madinat Jumeirah ■ 04 366 8888 ■ www.madinatjumeirah. com ■ DDD

The opulent Al Qasr ("the palace" in Arabic) is graced with enormous wooden doors, elegant arches and Moroccan stonework. Throughout you'll find mashrabiya screens, Moroccan lamps and terracotta urns. There's a gorgeous white-sand beach and views of Mina A'Salam and Burj Al Arab Jumeirah.

Atlantis, The Palm

MAP B1 ■ The Palm Jumeirah, Dubai ■ 04 426 0000 ■ www. atlantisthepalm.com ■ DDD

Located at the top of the Palm Jumeirah, this vast complex has a wide choice of rooms, most with views over the Gulf. The ultimate in luxury, however, are the Lost Chambers suites with underwater views into the lagoon. Among the many facilities are a water park, a dolphinarium and a kids' club, making it ideal for families (see p84).

Burj Al Arab Jumeirah

MAP C1 ■ Jumeirah Rd ■ 04 301 7777 ■ www. jumeirah.com ■ DDD

Jutting into the sea, this iconic property provides the ultimate in personal attention – from your arrival in a Rolls Royce, to the staff greeting you in the flamboyant foyer with welcome refreshments, cold towels, incense and dates, to the personal butler in your duplex suite. The interior is a little gaudy for some tastes, but the

spectacular coastal views, especially from the Skyview Bar, make up for it.

Jumeirah Zabeel Saray

MAP B1 ■ Palm Jumeirah ■ 04 453 0000 ■ www. jumeirah.com ■ DDD

This extravagant hotel often offers affordable rates. The outside looks like an Ottoman palace, while the interior boasts an array of restaurants, bars and public areas in a range of styles. A beach plus infinity pool completes the package.

Mina A'Salam

MAP C2 ■ Madinat Jumeirah ■ 04 366 8888 ■ www.madinatjumeirah. com ■ DDD

The old-Arabian architecture of Mina A'Salam is inspired by the ancient towers of Yemen and Saudi Arabia as well as by the windtower architecture of Dubai's Al Fahidi area. Rooms feature inlaid furniture, rich Oriental lamps and Arabesque-patterned prints and tiles. Lattice balconies overlook the man-made waterways and splendid beach.

One&Only Royal Mirage

MAP B2 ■ Al Sufouh Rd, Dubai Marina ■ 04 399 9999 ■ www. oneandonlyresorts.com ■ DDD

One of the world's most romantic resorts, this exotic Moroccan-inspired hotel is set in lush palm-filled gardens with serene ponds. The white-sand beach is lined with elegant white umbrellas and regal, private VIP canopies overlooking the Palm Jumeirah.

Ritz Carlton
MAP B2 ■ The Walk at JBR, Dubai Marina ■ 04 399 4000 ■ www.ritzcarlton.com ■ DDD
This sumptuous hotel lives up to the reputation of this renowned chain, with lots of marble, chandeliers, Persian carpets and fresh flowers everywhere. Its palm-filled gardens and white-sand beach are stunning.

Inexpensive and Moderate Hotels in Dubai

Ahmedia Heritage Guesthouse
MAP K1 ■ Near Al Ahmadiya School, Deira souk ■ 04 225 0085 ■ www.heritagedubaihotels.com ■ D
Book here for a real taste of heritage flavour. Located on the Deira side of the creek, this guesthouse has spacious, traditionally styled rooms in a bright courtyard building.

Arabian Courtyard Hotel & Spa
MAP K2 ■ Al Fahidi St, opposite Dubai Museum, Bur Dubai ■ 04 351 9111 ■ www.arabiancourtyard.com ■ D
Views of this historic area from the Arabian Courtyard are some of Dubai's most fascinating. The Arabian-inspired rooms are spacious and the staff friendly.

Barjeel Heritage Guest House
MAP J1 ■ Shindagha, Bur Dubai ■ 04 354 4424 ■ www.heritagedubaihotels.com ■ D
Attractive heritage guesthouse in a stunning setting on the Shindagha waterfront. The nine rooms are attractively decorated in traditional Arabian style and there's also a good little in-house restaurant serving local-style food.

Golden Sands Hotel Apartments
MAP J2 ■ Al Mankhool St, Bur Dubai ■ 04 355 5553 ■ www.goldensandsdubai.com ■ D
Comfortable self-catering accommodation in studios with kitchenettes, close to supermarkets and shops in Bur Dubai. All rooms have a TV and telephone. Free shuttle bus to Jumeirah.

Ibis World Trade Centre Hotel
MAP E6 ■ Next to the Dubai Convention and Exhibition Centre, Sheikh Zayed Rd ■ 04 332 4444 ■ www.ibishotel.com ■ D
One of Dubai's better bargains, the Ibis offers small, clean and stylish rooms in an excellent midtown location. The catch, however, is that there's no service or extras for this price – don't expect someone to help with your bags. The hotel restaurant, Cubo, offers decent Italian fare.

Orient Guest House
MAP K2 ■ Al Fahidi Roundabout, Bur Dubai ■ 04 353 4448 ■ www.heritagedubaihotels.com ■ D
This delightful boutique hotel is situated in a renovated courtyard building in the historic Al Fahidi neighbourhood. The traditional rooms with high ceilings are decorated in Arabian and Indian style and the quiet courtyards are wonderful for relaxing in after a hot day's sightseeing.

Raintree Hotel
MAP L5 ■ Garhoud Rd, Deira ■ 04 209 5111 ■ www.raintreehotels dubai.com ■ D
Centrally located behind Deira city centre, this smart and competitively priced modern hotel offers excellent service, plus a gym and rooftop pool.

XVA
MAP K2 ■ Al Fahidi ■ 04 353 5383 ■ www.xvahotel.com ■ D
This elegant hotel in a restored courtyard house is full of atmosphere. The stylish hotel rooms are minimalist in design. Don't expect any extras here; but who needs them when you can hear the call-to-prayer echoing through the streets?

Four Points Sheraton
MAP J2 ■ Khalid Bin Al-Waleed Rd ■ 04 397 7444 ■ www.four pointsburdubai.com ■ DD
Convenient for Bur Dubai souks, Dubai Museum, the Al Fahidi neighbourhood and Burjuman Mall shopping, this standard hotel is popular with business travellers and tourists on stopovers.

Jumeirah Creekside Hotel
MAP E2 ■ Garhoud ■ 04 230 8555 ■ www.jumeirah.com ■ DD
Furnished with modern art and contemporary designs, this wonderful hotel offers top-notch facilities and gorgeous views of the creek.

Luxury Hotels in Abu Dhabi

Eastern Mangroves Hotel & Spa

MAP V3 ■ Salam St ■ 02 656 1000 ■ www.abu-dhabi.anantara.com ■ DD
Opulent waterfront resort in a spectacular location overlooking extensive coastal mangrove swamps – a winning combination of luxury and nature. The Arabian-style interior is nicely done, and there's also a gorgeous spa and several fine restaurants.

Fairmont Bab al Bahr

MAP V4 ■ Between the Bridges ■ 02 654 3333 ■ www.fairmont.com/babalbahr ■ DD
Huge but homely five-star hotel, with sumptuous rooms and views over a creek and Sheikh Zayed Mosque. All rooms have lavish bathrooms, plus there's a fitness centre and a private beach. Chef Marco Pierre White has made his mark here with two restaurants.

Intercontinental Abu Dhabi

MAP N2 ■ Al Bateen St ■ 02 666 6888 ■ www.intercontinental.com ■ DD
Spacious and relaxing five-star option set at the quiet western end of Downtown. The idyllic beach and huge pool are a major draw, as is the brilliant collection of in-house restaurants.

Jumeirah at Etihad Towers

MAP N2 ■ Corniche Rd West ■ 02 811 5555 ■ www.jumeirah.com ■ DD
One of Abu Dhabi's smartest addresses, occupying one of the five soaring Etihad Towers. Rooms boast crisp contemporary design and all mod-cons, and there's also a large private beach with three pools.

Park Hyatt Abu Dhabi

MAP V2 ■ Saadiyat Island ■ 02 407 1234 ■ www.abudabi.parkhyatt.com ■ DD
Located on a 9-km (6-mile) stretch of beach, with its own landscaped garden, the Park Hyatt has become one of Abu Dhabi's most desired locations. It is just a short drive from the city, but a world away in terms of tranquility.

Shangri-La Qaryat Al Beri

MAP V4 ■ Qaryat Al Beri ■ 02 509 8888 ■ www.shangri-la.com ■ DD
Lavish Arabian-style hotel with rooms overlooking either the long private beach, or one of the swimming pools. It also has a lovely spa and fine restaurants, while all the amenities of the Souk Qaryat al Beri (see p97) are right next door.

Sofitel Abu Dhabi Corniche

MAP V4 ■ Corniche Road East ■ 02 813 7777 ■ sofitel.com ■ DD
One of Downtown's newest and most alluring hotels, with plenty of cool contemporary style. The Art Deco-inspired high-rise building offers brilliant views from the upper floors, while the chic Jazz 'n Fizz Bar has become established as one of the area's most fashionable hangouts.

St Regis Saadiyat Island Resort

MAP V2 ■ Saadiyat Island ■ 02 498 8888 ■ www.stregissaadiyatisland.com ■ DD
Sprawling modern resort on a long and idyllic stretch of Saadiyat Island beach. The monumental mock-Tuscan design is a little overwhelming, but the lush grounds create an enjoyably rustic atmosphere, while facilities include several excellent restaurants and a stunning pool.

Yas Viceroy

MAP W4 ■ Yas Island ■ 02 656 0000 ■ www.viceroyhotelsandresorts.com ■ DD
Upmarket (but often surprisingly affordable) hotel at the heart of the swanky Yas Marina development. Built directly over the F1 Grand Prix circuit and wrapped in a spectacular illuminated canopy roof, the hotel is one of the city's most memorable modern buildings. Inside, everything is the height of contemporary cool, from the immaculate rooms to a string of very chic restaurants and bars.

Emirates Palace

MAP N1 ■ The Corniche West ■ 02 690 9000 ■ www.emiratespalace.com ■ DDD
Choose from amongst the Coral, Pearl and Diamond Rooms, Khaleej Suites or Palace Suites at Abu Dhabi's grandest hotel. All the rooms feature wide plasma TVs and extras such as welcome cocktails, flowers and fruit in the room, plus butler service.

For a key to hotel price categories see p112

Inexpensive and Moderate Hotels in Abu Dhabi

Al Ain Palace Hotel
MAP S2 ■ Corniche Road East ■ 02 679 4777 ■ www.alainpalacehotel.com ■ D

One of the oldest hotels in the city, it may look its age but still enjoys large, comfortable rooms, a friendly atmosphere and competitive prices. It also boasts a surprisingly extensive selection of places to eat and drink, making it an attractive option for those who don't feel like heading out after a hot day's sightseeing.

Hilton Abu Dhabi
MAP N2 ■ Corniche Rd West ■ 02 681 1900 ■ www.hilton.com ■ D

Long a favourite of Abu Dhabi's expats for its excellent restaurants and bars, this hotel posseses beautiful swimming pools and Corniche-front beach, lined with shady palm trees – it also offers an array of water sports. Choose from a variety of spacious and comfortable rooms that come with many little extras – some even offer Gulf views.

Hyatt Capital Gate
MAP U3 ■ Capital Gate ■ 02 596 1234 ■ www.abudhabicapitalgate.hyatthotels.hyatt.com ■ D

A very smart but also competitively priced hotel in the famously leaning Capital Gate tower (see p99). It boasts cool modern rooms and amazing views from its higher floors. There's also a great spa and stunning pool.

Mercure Abu Dhabi Centre
MAP R2 ■ Hamdan St ■ 02 633 3555 ■ www.mercure.com ■ D

Centrally located, this old hotel looks worn around the edges but is a good choice thanks to its rock-bottom rates and brilliantly central location. Good street views from higher floors.

Millennium Hotel
MAP S1 ■ Khalifa St ■ 02 614 6000 ■ www.millenniumhotels.com ■ D

This swanky but very reasonably priced hotel has elegant and expansive rooms with splendid views over the Corniche, Lulu Island and out to sea. Ideally positioned for Downtown sight-seeing, there is also a small swimming pool.

Le Royal Meridien
MAP T2 ■ Khalifa St ■ 02 674 2020 ■ www.lemeridien.com ■ D

All the beautifully appointed rooms at this contemporary hotel have sublime views of both the Corniche and the Arabian Sea, and there are a couple of nice pools concealed amongst the peaceful walled gardens.

Sheraton Abu Dhabi Resort & Towers
MAP T1 ■ Corniche Rd East, Tourist Club area ■ 02 677 3333 ■ www.sheraton.com/abudhabi ■ D

Set right on the Corniche, there are good water and leisure activities at this resort hotel, and the beachside sheesha spot is lovely. Eat at the excellent restaurants on site.

Southern Sun
MAP T1 ■ Al Mina St ■ 02 818 4888 ■ www.tsogosunhotels.com/hotels/abu-dhabi ■ D

Very smart but affordable modern hotel in a central Downtown location. Facilities include a gym and rooftop pool, plus there are a couple of top-class restaurants

Traders Hotel Quaryat al Beri
MAP V4 ■ Khor al Maqta ■ 02 510 8888 ■ www.shangri-la.com/abudhabi/traders ■ D

Set in a lovely location overlooking Maqta Creek, this above-average mid-range hotel (part of the Shangri-La hotel group) has very smooth service and, for the price, a surprising amount of style. Modern rooms and public areas are decorated with colourful minimalist decor, and there's also a small pool plus private beach.

Beach Rotana
MAP T2 ■ 10th St, Al Zahiyah ■ 02 697 9000 ■ www.rotana.com/beachrotana ■ DD

Vast resort-style hotel in the heart of Downtown, with smart modern rooms, a small stretch of beach, private beach club and spa, stunning Al Maryah Island views, and one of the city's best selections of places to eat and drink.

Beyond the Cities

Fujairah Rotana Resort and Spa
E99 coastal highway, Fujairah ■ 09 244 9888 ■ www.rotana.com ■ D

On beautiful Al Aqah Beach, this luxury east

coast resort offers a blissful beachside break from the big cities, with upmarket style and facilities for well under the price of similar hotels in either Dubai or Abu Dhabi. It lies close to the equally large, though less overpowering, Le Méridien Al Aqah.

Al Ain Rotana
120th St, Al Ain ▪ 03 754 5111 ▪ www.rotana.com/ alainrotana ▪ DD
The best hotel in Al Ain, centrally located and with a fine array of five-star facilities. The lovely gardens and pools are great for daytime lazing, while the hotel's excellent restaurants, including the Arabian-style Min Zaman and the lively Trader Vics, are enjoyable places to relax after dark.

Anantara Qasr Al Sarab
A 90-minute drive from Abu Dhabi ▪ 02 886 2088 ▪ www.qasralsarab. anantara.com ▪ DD
Looking like something out of Lawrence of Arabia, this magical fortress-style resort sits majestically in the middle of the desert surrounding the spectacular Liwa Oasis, the UAE's finest area of unspoilt wilderness. Rooms feature five-star luxuries and there are private villas, each with a pool and butler service.

Desert Palm
Al Ain highway ▪ 04 323 8888 ▪ www.desertpalm. peraquum.com ▪ DD
On the fringes of Dubai, around a 20-minute drive from the airport, the intimate little Desert Palm resort offers an

idyllic retreat from the hectic pace of urban life. The superbly equipped rooms come with private pool and all mod-cons, while the surrounding polo fields create an enjoyably country atmosphere and the spa is second to none.

Kempinski Hotel Ajman
Ajman ▪ 06 714 5555 ▪ www.kempinski.com ▪ DD
In the tiny emirate of Ajman, just north of Sharjah, the Kempinski offers a convenient retreat from the big-city bustle of nearby Dubai. Despite this beachfront resort's dated appearance, the hotel remains profoundly relaxing, with fine gardens, a beautiful pool and a private white-sand beach perfect for idle lounging.

Le Méridien Al Aqah Beach Resort
E99 coastal highway, Fujairah ▪ 09 244 9000 ▪ www.lemeridien-alaqah.com ▪ DD
On idyllic Al Aqah Beach with the Hajar Mountains forming the backdrop, this towering resort is one of the east coast's major landmarks, with five-star facilities and huge grounds. It's a good place to set up diving trips.

Al Maha Desert Resort and Spa
Dubai Desert Conservation Reserve (60km/37 miles from Dubai) ▪ 04 832 9900 ▪ www.al-maha.com ▪ DDD
Idyllic desert retreat in the heart of the Dubai Desert Conservation Reserve. Rare wildlife

roams the grounds, giving the whole place almost the feel of an African bush camp, while the lavishly appointed tented suites offer plenty of luxury, including private plunge pools.

Anantara Sir Bani Yas Islands Resort
Sir Bani Yas Island (a 90-minute drive from Abu Dhabi) ▪ 02 656 1399 ▪ www.sir-bani-yas-island.anantara.com ▪ DDD
One of the UAE's most magical – and unusual – places to stay. The resort is located on Sir Bani Yas Island, which was transformed by Sheikh Zayed in the 1970s into a remarkable nature reserve teeming with wildlife ranging from indigenous Arabian oryx to prancing giraffes. The main resort itself is one of the country's most palatial, and there are also two separate luxury eco-lodges – Al Yamm and Al Sahel – deeper inside the reserve.

Bab Al Shams Desert Resort and Spa
Emirates Rd ▪ 04 809 6498 ▪ www.meydan hotels.com/babalshams ▪ DDD
Spectacular resort hidden away in the desert, just a 45-minute drive from Dubai. Built in the style of a traditional Arabian fort, the resort has top-class facilities including a stunning infinity pool and the memorable Al Hadheerah open-air desert restaurant. This is a great place to enjoy desert activities, such as camel riding and falconry displays.

For a key to hotel price categories see p112

General Index

Acknowledgments

Authors
Lara Dunston has authored several guides to Dubai and the UAE and regularly writes travel features for magazines and newspapers around the world.

Sarah Monaghan lived in Dubai for five years where she edited its leading women's magazine *Emirates Woman*. She now contributes to travel features and international publications.

Additional contributor
Gavin Thomas

Publishing Director Georgina Dee

Publisher Vivien Antwi

Design Director Phil Ormerod

Editorial Sophie Adam, Ankita Awasthi Tröger, Michelle Crane, Alice Fewery, Rachel Fox, Sally Schafer, Akanksha Siwach, Jackie Staddon

Cover Design: Richard Czapnik

Design Tessa Bindloss, Rahul Kumar, Marisa Renzullo, Ankita Sharma, Vinita Venugopal

Picture Research Subhadeep Biswas, Taiyaba Khatoon, Ellen Root

Cartography Suresh Kumar, James McDonald, Casper Morris, Reetu Pandey

DTP Jason Little

Production Luca Bazzoli

Factchecker Suha Halaseh

Proofreader Leena Lane

Indexer Hilary Bird

First edition created by Quadrum Solutions, Mumbai.

Picture Credits
The publisher would like to thank the following for their kind permission to reproduce their photographs:
Key: a-above; b-below/bottom; c-centre; f-far; l-left; r-right; t-top
123RF.com: Luciano Mortula 93cl; pio3 73cla; Fedor Selivanov 92b; Oleg Zhukov 26clb.

Abu Dhabi Desert Challenge: 39tr.

Alamy Stock Photo: age fotostock 14cla; arabianEye FZ LLC 13tr; Asia Photopress 27tl; Kairi Aun 33bl; Tibor Bognar 61cl; Yvette Cardozo 14br; China Span / Keren Su 2tr, 34-35bl; Dallet-Alba 64cla; eye35.pix 84b; Stuart Forster 98clb; Godong 21tl; Hemis 47br, 66c; imageBROKER 59tl; John Kellerman 4crb; Feroz Khan 11br; LH Images 10ca, 18bl; Nino Marcutti 7cr, 44b; Iain Masterton 71br, 85cla, 91br; Middle East 16cla; Lewis Oliver 10clb; Prisma Bildagentur AG 3tl, 4cr, 56-7; Robertharding 3tr, 4t, 96tl, 102-3; Urbanmyth 98t; WorldTravel 65tr.

Armani Hotel: 12clb.

Art Space: 38-9.

Asha's: 69br.

Atlantis The Palm – Aquaventure: 42t.

Atlantis, The Palm: 41b, 84tl, Lost Chambers 83b.

AWL Images: Peter Adams 2tl, 8-9; Walter Bibikow 65b; Alan Copson 4clb; Danita Delimont Stock 15bc; Norbert Eisele-Hein 4cl; Nick Ledger 4b.

Burj Al Arab: 11tr, 24cr, 25tl, 25cra; Skyview Bar 48t.

Burj Khalifa: 12-3.

Coffee Museum: 18-9, 52bl.

Dreamstime.com: Altayebamer 51tr; Cristian Andriana 54-5, 55t; Badahos 11cr; Beijing Hetuchuangyi Images Co. Ltd . 22-3; Carabiner 79cla; Dvrcan 33tl; Elnur 28cl; Gmv 45cl; Laszlo Halasi 13bl; Ilonawellington 20-1; Joyshuai 77br; Patryk Kosmider 30-1, 52t, 97tr; Lexandr Lexandrovich 32clb; Manowar1973 6br, 51cl, 83ca; Miramcor 72b; Luciano Mortula 10tr, 28-9; Manoj Mundapat 54c; Outcast85 94cla; Photobac 88-9; Pivart 71tr; Romrodinka 76cl; Eq Roy 58cla; Mariia Savoskula 33crb; Seqoya 24-5; Konstantin Stepanenko 4cla; Petr Švec 28br, 82ca; Swisshippo 14-5,15tr, 30bl; TasFoto 17bl, 50tl; Topdeq 10cl; Typhoonski 53tr, 90cl, 99bl; Thor Jorgen Udvang 44c; Shao Weiwei 11clb; Oleg Zhukov 11cla, 60bl.

Dubai Creek Golf & Yacht Club: 16-7, 60t.

Emaar Properties: Burj Khalifa Lake 71tl.

Emirates Palace Abu Dhabi: Sayad 95cra.

Emirates Tower: 70cl.

Getty Images: AFP 37tr; Jon Arnold 66tr; Allan Baxter 91t; Mark Daffey 78tl; Pascal Deloche 29tl; Oliver Furrer 44tl; Matilde Gattoni 47tl; John Harper 78b; Kami Kami 92cla; AFP / Karim Sahib 20clb; Dan Kitwood 42bl; Sebastiaan Kroes 94br; Jean-Pierre Lescourret 68t; Maremagnum 26-7; Iain Masterton 72tl; Chris Mellor 67bl; Tuul and Bruno Morandi 10br; Francois Nel 45tr; Frans Sellies 53cbm; Sylvain Sonnet 17tl, 18ca; David Steele 59br; Keren Su 36tl; Rudy Sulgan 27br; Jochen Tack 31tr; ullstein bild 77t.

iStockphoto.com: Frankvanden Bergh 32-3; Dblight 37bl; Chandra Dhas 55crb; Dr Doru 37cla; naes 1; Serts 36bl; Shao Weiwei 31bl.

Johnny Rockets: 86bl.

Jumeirah Zabeel Saray: 40clb.

JW Marriott Marquis Hotel Dubai: Vault 74c.

Karma Kafé: 75bl.

Madinat Jumeirah: Bahri Bar 49clb, 81cra; Shimmers 49tr.

Mezlai: 46cla.

One&Only Royal Mirage: 41tl, 46b; The Rooftop 48clb; Tagine 87cla.

Park Hyatt Dubai / The Terrace: 62clb.

Phocal Media: 21crb, 29crb.

Radisson Blu Hotel / The China Club: 63cla.

Raffles Dubai: 40br.

Robert Harding Picture Library: Michael DeFreitas 50b.

Sega Republic: 43clb.

Souk Madinat Jumeirah: 80b.

The Third Line: 38cl.

Towers Rotana Dubai: Long's Bar 74tr.

XVA Gallery, Café & Hotel: 19br; Nathan Root 38tr.

Y Bar: 100t.

Yas Viceroy Abu Dhabi: Atayeb 101br.

Cover

Front and spine: **Getty Images:** Rudy Sulgan.
Back: **Dreamstime.com:** Ajandali.

Pull Out Map Cover

Getty Images: Rudy Sulgan.

All other images © Dorling Kindersley
For further information see:
www.dkimages.com

Printed and bound in China

First American Edition, 2007
Published in the United States by
DK Publishing, 345 Hudson Street,
New York, New York 10014

Copyright 2007, 2017 © Dorling
Kindersley Limited

A Penguin Random House Company

17 18 19 20 10 9 8 7 6 5 4 3 2 1

**Reprinted with revisions 2008, 2010, 2012,
2014, 2017**

Published in Great Britain by Dorling
Kindersley Limited.

A catalog record for this book is available
from the Library of Congress.

ISSN 1479-344X
ISBN 978-1-4654-6125-4

MIX
Paper from
responsible sources
FSC™ C018179

*As a guide to abbreviations in visitor information
blocks: **Adm** = admission charge; **DA** = disabled
access; **D** = dinner; **L** = lunch.*

Phrase Book

In an Emergency

Help!	*Enjedooni*
Stop	*Wak-kaf*
Can you call a doctor?	*Momkin tatlob tabeeb?*
Can you call an ambulance?	*Momkin tatlob el es'aaf?*
Can you call the police?	*Momkin tatlob el shorta?*
Can you call the fire brigade?	*Momkin tatlob el etfaa?*
Where is the nearest hospital?	*Wayn aqrab mostashfa?*
Is there a telephone here?	*Ako telefoon huna?*

Useful Words and Phrases

Yes	*Na-am*
No	*Laa*
Hello	*Salaam alaikum*
Goodbye	*Ma'aa al salaama*
See you later	*Ela al lekaa*
Excuse me	*'Afwan*
Sorry (said by man)	*Aasif*
Sorry (said by woman)	*Aasifa*
Thank you	*Shakereen*
Please	*Luw tasma`h*
Peace be upon you	*Al salaam 'alaikum*
Peace be upon you (as response)	*Alaikum al salaam*
Good morning	*Sabaa`h al khayr*
Good evening	*Masaa-o al khayr*
Good night	*Tosbihoona ala khayr*
Pleased to meet you	*Ya ahleen*
How are you?	*Keef al'haal?*
I'm fine	*Zeen*
I don't understand	*Ma afham*
What did he say?	*Shenu kaal?*
Do you speak English?	*Ta'hki enkleezi?*
Does anyone speak English?	*Aku 'hada ye'hkee enkleezi?*
Have you got a table for...?	*Aku taawila hug ...?*
I would like to reserve a table	*Areed a'hjiz taawila*
Can I have the bill please?	*Al 'hesaab luw tasma'h*
I am vegetarian	*Ana nabaati*
God willing	*Inshaal-la*
No problem	*Maafi moshkila*
big	*kabeer*
small	*sageer*
hot	*'haar*
cold	*baarid*
bad	*say-ye'e*
good	*tay-yeb*
open	*maftoo'h*
closed	*mesak-kar*
on the right	*'ala al yameen*
on the left	*'ala al yasaar*
near	*kareeb*
far	*ba'eed*
men's toilet	*twalet hug al rejaal*
ladies' toilet	*twalet hug al 'hareem*
a little	*kaleel*
a lot	*waajed*

Making a Telephone Call

Hello	*Aloo*
I'd like to speak to...	*Areed akal-lim...*
This is...	*Ana...*
I'll call back later	*Raa'h at-tasel ba'adeen*
Please say ... called	*Khab-birho an-na... et-tasal*

In a Hotel

hotel	*fondok*
Do you have a room?	*Ladaykom 'hojra?*
I have a reservation	*Endi 'hajz*
With bathroom	*Bee 'ham-maam*
single room	*'hojra fardiy-ya*
double room	*'hojra le etneen*
porter	*natoor*
shower	*dosh*
key	*meftaa'h*

Sightseeing

art gallery	*ma'arad luw'haat faney-ya*
beach	*shaate'e*
bus station	*muwgaf el baahs*
district	*mentakaa*
entrance	*madkhal*
exit	*makhraj*
garden	*'hadeeka*
guide	*morshid*
guided tour	*morshid al juwla*
map	*khaarta*
mosque	*jaame'a*
museum	*mut'haf*
park	*motanaz-zah*
river	*naher*
taxi	*taksi*
ticket	*tathkara*
tourist office	*maktab seyaa'hi*
Please put the (taxi) meter on	*Luw tasma'h, daw-war al 'ad-daad*
How much is it to...?	*Kam raah tekal-lafni ela...?*
Please take me to (this address)	*Khothni ela (haaza al 'onwaan)*

Shopping

How much is it?	*Kam floos?*
I'd like...	*Areed*
This one	*Haaza*
Do you accept credit cards?	*Hal takbaloon kredit kaard?*
That's too much	*Haaza waayed*
I'll give you...	*Ana raa'h a'ateek...*
I'll take it	*Raa'h aakhdoh*
market	*sook*
expensive	*ghaali*
cheap	*rakhees*
chemist's	*saydalaani*

Menu Decoder

'aish	rice
'aseer	fruit juice
bedoon	without
bee	with
beera	beer
beez	egg
beez maslook	hard-boiled egg
beriaani al dajaaj	chicken biryani
beriaani al lahem	meat biryani
beriaani al robiaan	shrimp biryani
beriaani samak	fish biryani (with bones)
bolti	spiced tilapia (fish) grilled and served whole
da-en	mutton
dajaaj	chicken

faakiha — fruit
falaafel — vegetarian burger made with chickpeas

fee al forn — roasted
fulful — white pepper
fulful aswad — black pepper
gabgab — steamed crab
guhwa — bitter Arabic coffee

haleeb — milk
halwa — Turkish delight with cardamom
ham-moor — local fish that tastes like snapper
ham-moor magli — deep-fried hammoor
harees — gruel cooked in beef stock
heel — cardamom
holo — sweet
kabaab — kebab
kabsa — dish of rice, meat/chicken, dried lemon and saffron
kabsat dajaaj — dish of rice, chicken, dry lemon and saffron
kabsat lahem — dish of rice, meat, dry lemon and saffron
kereem — cream
khal — vinegar made from molasses
khamr — wine
khoboz — bread
khoboz jabaab — large spiced pancakes with cardamom
khoboz shaami — pita bread
khoboz tost — toast
kofta — grilled meatballs
koozi — lamb
koskos — plain couscous
maglee — fried
malh — salt
marag — spiced meat/chicken stock
marag dajaaj — chicken stock
marag lahem — beef stock
mashroob ghaazi — soft drink
mashwi — grilled
mashwi ala el fa`hm — barbecued over coal
masloog — boiled
mohal-li senaa-ee — sweetener
moham-mas — toasted
nabeez — wine
neskafee — coffee
orz — rice
orz bil zafaraan — rice with saffron
robyaan — large grilled shrimp
shai — tea
shawirma — doner kebab
suk-kar — sugar
sulsa — tomato purée cooked in stock
tahye motawas-sit — medium
tshaaw meen dajaaj — chicken chowmein
tshaaw meen lahem — beef chowmein
tshaaw meen samak — seafood chowmein

tshoop sooy — chop suey
wajba khafeefa — snack
zaatar — thyme
zangabeel — ginger powder
zobod — butter

Numbers

1	*waa'hid*
2	*etneen*
3	*thalaatha*
4	*arba'aa*
5	*khamsa*
6	*sit-ta*
7	*saba'a*
8	*thamaaneya*
9	*tes'aa*
10	*'ashra*
11	*'hedaash*
12	*etnaash*
13	*talat-taash*
14	*arba'-taash*
15	*khamastaash*
16	*sit-taash*
17	*saba'ataash*
18	*tamantaash*
19	*tesa'ataash*
20	*eshreen*
21	*waa'hid wa eshreen*
30	*thalaatheen*
40	*arbe'een*
50	*khamseen*
60	*sit-teen*
70	*sab'een*
80	*thamaneen*
90	*tes'een*
100	*me-aa*
1000	*alf*

Time

Today	*el yoom*
yesterday	*el bariha*
tomorrow	*baaker*
morning	*sabaa'h*
afternoon	*zaheera*
evening	*masaa*
night	*lail*
now	*al 'heen*
tonight	*el laila*
minute	*dageega*
hour	*sa'aa*
week	*osboo'a*
month	*shahr*
year	*'aam*

Days of the Week

Monday	*al ethneen*
Tuesday	*al thulathaa*
Wednesday	*al arbe'a*
Thursday	*al khamees*
Friday	*al jomo'aa*
Saturday	*al sabet*
Sunday	*al a'had*

Months

January	*yanaayer*
February	*febraayer*
March	*maaris*
April	*abreel*
May	*maayo*
June	*yonyo*
July	*yolyo*
August	*agostos*
September	*sebtamber*
October	*oktoobar*
November	*noovambir*
December	*deesambir*

Dubai Selected Street Index

Abu Dhabi Selected Street Index